ːs for ... ne 2

ːnts reminds us that navigating difficult challenges
possibilities for growth, change, and forward
ries are a reminder of the strength found within

ɔold
Picasso Painted a Snowman

Courage. There is no book more poignant to read
ning Point Moments, which not only encouraged me
y own life but captivated me with every turn of the
add this book to your shortlist."

Murphy
f the Best-Selling Memoir, *Gingered*

ıen a book comes along with just the right message
ıe. *Turning Point Moments* is one of these exceptional
as assembled an incredible group of contributors
the narratives but also the techniques and mental
we think about what life delivers us and how we
t to experience more days where you are filled
and drive, the inspiring stories in this book will
ıttitude of gratitude."

ı (Dempster)
ged Consulting in the Digital Age

offers deep insights on our vulnerabilities as
ːes reflection to become our better self."

ıis
Performance LLC

"Through a collection of heartfelt narratives, *Turn*
illuminates the transformative power of seizing piv
taking charge of our lives. With each story, we are
incredible potential within ourselves to shape our d

~ Jamie Harding
CEO and Founder, TheatrixHD – Home to the
music, arts, and entertainment

"If you enjoyed and learned anything from the book C
Soul, you'll love *Turning Point Moments*. These stories
and great learning experiences for us all! Every in
arisen from a serious setback. The advice provided
survivors is invaluable. Do yourself a favor and make
your library."

~ Rachel E.
Content Creation Manager

"These stories reflect my own feelings. Having this
share their experiences is an inspiration for all h
discover their true selves and live a life of purpose."

~ Wally Kozak
Sports Leadership Ambassador, serving the
"Good of the Game"

"If you're struggling to navigate through tough times
stories will set you on the path of healing, hope, and

~ Claudine Paquet
Author, *BY EXAMPLE: Educate with Ease and C*
Fear or Guilt

"Never has there been a more critical time in human history to be aware that our turning points are potent activators of who we're meant to become, rather than the status quo of who we've been. Each of these challenging moments, while it may feel traumatic or painful, is the stimulus to let go of something that no longer serves. These inspiring stories depict challenges as a wake-up call to uncover our Golden Thread of purpose, so that we may birth the next version of us that calls us to be birthed. A must-read!"

~ Holly Woods PhD
Best-selling Author, *The Golden Thread: Where to Find Purpose in the Stages of Your Life*

"The heartfelt stories written by these authors are deeply personal, and a valuable tool for anyone experiencing a turning point moment in their own life. Their courage helps you know that you, too, can shine through any challenge."

~ Carmen Swick, Author

"This book contains many amazing transformational experiences that reveal the sudden realization that a life of 'accumulation' often lacks fulfillment. These stories about the search for purpose, fulfillment, and the ultimate destination of Personal Mastery are worth taking time to sit down and read."

~ Tom Wentz
President, Corporate Performance Systems

TURNING POINT MOMENTS

VOLUME 2

COMPILED BY
CHRISTINE KLOSER

Capucia LLC
211 Pauline Drive #513
York, PA 17402

www.capuciapublishing.com

Send questions to: support@capuciapublishing.com

Paperback ISBN: 978-1-954920-72-9
eBook ISBN: 978-1-954920-73-6
Library of Congress Control Number: 2022910589

Cover Design: fingerplus | Agus Budiyono
Layout: Ranilo Cabo
Editor and Proofreader: Karen Burton
Book Midwife: Carrie Jareed

Printed in the United States of America

Capucia LLC is proud to be a part of the Tree Neutral® program. Tree Neutral offsets the number of trees consumed in the production and printing of this book by taking proactive steps such as planting trees in direct proportion to the number of trees used to print books. To learn more about Tree Neutral, please visit treeneutral.com.

100% of all publisher proceeds from the sale of this book will go toward supporting people who are experiencing turning point moments in their life through contributions to organizations like Pandemic of Love, The Teen Project, and National Alliance on Mental Health.

To everyone who has ever experienced a turning point moment in their life

CONTENTS

INTRODUCTION

The turning point in the life of those who succeed usually comes at the moment of some crisis.
—Napoleon Hill

Welcome to *Turning Point Moments—Volume Two.* We are so excited this book crossed your path, and you chose to pick up a copy and crack open the cover. My guess is—like the contributing authors—you are familiar with the significance of turning point moments in your life.

Perhaps as you read this, you've just come through a challenging situation with a renewed sense of faith and hope. Or, maybe you're in the middle of one of those gut-wrenching turning points. Perhaps you have a strong sense that one of these life-changing moments is lurking around the corner waiting for you, but you just don't know what it is yet.

No matter where you are right now on your life's journey, I trust that since you're here—taking time to read this book—you believe in the power and possibility of turning point moments to help you create a better and more fulfilling life.

While the difficulties of turning point experiences sometimes make us doubt if we can go on another day, somewhere in the depths of your being, you *know* that good things can unfold as you navigate and grow through these impactful situations. The important thing—and what you'll read about on the pages—is the resolve to know that what you're going through isn't something that's happening *to* you, it's something that is happening *for* you.

It doesn't matter if you're a leading-edge entrepreneur, schoolteacher, parent, rocket scientist, doctor, writer, healer, manager, salesperson, nurse, volunteer, retiree, or anything else; your life will bring you many of these pivotal moments. What you do with them and how you grow through them make all the difference.

These times we're living in are turning point moment times. You can't be alive on the planet right now and not in some way be conscious of the critical moments we are living in as a collective humanity. People ask, *What can I do? How can I make a difference?* One of the answers is to extract all the growth, healing, and transformation out of your personal turning point moments so you are a stronger, brighter, more resilient person who is shining that ray of hope and possibility for others in the world. We all need the reminder that we are strong enough to not only survive but thrive through these evolutionary times. Navigating the moments in our own life is how we grow that resiliency.

To that end, inside this book you'll get to know such people. My team and I feel blessed to have supported the contributors in this book to share their story. Some of these authors have wanted to get published for decades, and now they have done it with our help here at Capucia LLC. We've come together over the course of six months to birth this book for you. As you discover each contributor's story, you'll see why we consider it a blessing to call them our clients and friends on the journey.

Some chapters may make you cry, while others may make you chuckle. Some will seem unbelievable or *out there* while others may be touching reflections of your own turning point moment experience.

Our hope is that every chapter offers you a heartfelt reassurance that if they can do it (whatever the *it* is), you can too. If they can extract the good and use it to improve their lives, the same path is available for you.

So, as you read through this book, I invite you to be lifted by what you read and see some new possibilities for yourself, and for all people. I also invite you to embrace the great diversity of the contributing authors. Their ethnicities, religious beliefs, career paths, backgrounds, and journeys are as diverse as can be. Yet, as you will see on these pages, their hearts all stand for the same thing—using their turning point moments as a catalyst for positive change.

As you proceed through this book, feel free to read the chapters out of order. Chances are as you peruse the table of contents or randomly flip open the pages, you will receive exactly the message that is meant for you in that moment.

Above all else, let the stories in this book bathe you in possibility, hope, resolve, and inspiration to transform your turning point moment (large or small) into beautiful blessings for yourself and others.

On behalf of myself, my amazing team, and all the contributing authors, we send you our deepest blessings that these stories deliver the inspiration you need to help you create a life that works for you. And may your life cause a ripple effect of good in the world.

Blessings on your journey,

Christine Kloser
Founder and CEO, Get Your Book Done®
Founder and CEO, Capucia Publishing®

CHAPTER 1

Connecting the Dots

Christine Kloser

It was January 7, 2023, around 9:30 p.m. I was participating in an intensive transformational retreat with a small group of cherished women friends in York, Pennsylvania. At the end of the first day, I found myself curled up in a ball on the floor, sobbing from a place I didn't even know existed inside myself. It was in that moment when—for the first time in my fifty-six years on the planet—I deeply experienced how emotionally unsafe I have felt throughout my entire life.

I remember saying out loud to one of my friends, "I had no idea how unsafe I've felt." It was surprising. It was deep. I felt this new awareness in every cell of my being. It was painful. It was mind-numbing. It felt insurmountable at the time. And it was also the eye of the needle I needed to pass through to connect the dots and make sense of my life and career.

If you asked anyone who knew me, they most likely wouldn't have imagined this was the unconscious inner experience I had been living through. Heck, I couldn't imagine it either, and I was the one smack dab in the middle of it. How could I not see it? How did I miss this huge component that was part of my personal operating system? But soon after this eye-opening and cathartic moment of awakening and the safety I felt with one of my friends who held me and witnessed me through this turning point moment, everything started to make sense. All the dots that used to feel disjointed in my life began to connect right in front of my eyes.

Here's a snapshot of what I mean by disjointed. When everyone else at my college was vying for entry-level jobs in banking or insurance, I was planning the route I'd take to move 3,000 miles away from home to San Diego—a place I had never visited, where I didn't know anyone, had no job, and didn't know where I'd live or how I'd get there since my car had just broken down past the point of repair. One year later, I moved back to my home state of Connecticut to get a *real* job, only to move across the country again to Los Angeles just two years later.

At this point, the story gets interesting as Los Angeles is where I began my entrepreneurial journey—a place marked with so many *dots* that I never thought they'd ever make sense and come together. But with the help of my turning point moment discovery, they did.

You see, within months of landing in Los Angeles in 1991—where I first started out as a nanny caring for a five-year old boy whose mother died in childbirth and whose father was unable to truly take care of him—I had a *random* conversation with a friend in a hot tub. That conversation led to me becoming certified as a personal trainer and starting my own personal training business in which I took great care of amazing clients from celebrities like Reba McEntire to local business owners who remain dear friends thirty-plus years later.

Personal training, along with teaching group fitness classes, led me to discovering yoga and becoming a certified yoga instructor. That certification led me to teaching at one of the premier studies in Los Angeles for one of the world's top yoga instructors. This position opened a door that led me to being offered a space in one of my student's office buildings to run the personal training gym and yoga studio he had built out but had been empty for a couple years.

During this time, I also started facilitating transformational retreats for women in Lake Arrowhead, California, called the "Vision Weekend." A friend and I co-led these events, and we helped women create a vision for their lives and experience the breakthroughs they needed to live them.

The experience of going from a home-based fitness business to brick and mortar studio was far more challenging than I ever imagined. I scoured Los Angeles in search of a women's networking group to meet other like-minded women business owners, so I didn't feel so alone. I needed to know I wasn't the only one struggling. All I found were groups in which everyone was *great,* business was always *terrific*, and pressed suits and fancy business cards were the name of the game. So, I gave up looking.

Instead, I gathered my own small group of women friends for dinner one night—none of whom were business owners—to share my vision of a place where women entrepreneurs could come together and be real with each other. Let their hair down. Be honest about how they were doing. Ask for the support they needed and receive it. That group of five women in the back of a Chinese restaurant in west Los Angeles turned into a group of 500 women, and I then hosted dinners and seminars in hotel ballrooms.

What did all of this have to do with my career in the fitness industry? Stay tuned, I promise the dots will be connected.

This group was called the Network for Empowering Women Entrepreneurs, and the tagline was "Ignite Your Business and Fuel Your Soul." It was through that group that I landed in the world of book publishing. I had offered my husband help with publishing a book idea he had but wasn't convinced he'd bring his idea to life. He did. I had to figure out how to publish it. Once I knew what to do, I offered the women in my community the opportunity to contribute a chapter to my first anthology so I could help them get published too. Forty women said yes. That book was published and reviewed in *Entrepreneur Magazine* as one of the best books for women to read the summer after it came out.

Unbeknownst to me, this one anthology book (similar to the one you're reading right now) put me on a path of writing my own book called *The Freedom Formula*. This book launched a whole other business that helped people put "soul in their business and money in the bank," which I did for one year. I simultaneously developed my *Get Your Book Done* program to show people how to write their own transformational books. Over the past twenty years of coaching authors, I've since trained 90,000 people in 127 countries, personally published over 650 authors, and am blessed with the most phenomenal team that any CEO could ask for.

As a transformational author coach, I've also facilitated in-person and virtual events for thousands of people over the years, and I've hosted writing retreats in beautiful places like Costa Rica, the Bahamas, and Tulum, Mexico. I've witnessed lives change right in front of my eyes through the powerful process of writing a transformational book.

What did being an author coach and publisher have to do with the work I did building and supporting a community of women entrepreneurs? And what does all of this have to do with my first business in the fitness industry, or most recent product-focused company called Love Wraps, whose mission is to literally wrap the world in love one person at a time? And how does that all fit with me becoming a certified Groove Dance facilitator in my fifties? Everything felt so disjointed, disconnected, and out of whack. I loved it all, but it didn't make any sense.

Until that moment on the floor in January 2023 when I realized how emotionally unsafe I had felt my entire life. Creating safety for others had been the throughline of every iteration of my work in the world. Because I unconsciously knew how painful it was to feel unsafe, it turns out I was also naturally gifted at knowing intuitively exactly how to bring emotional safety to any situation—whether I was teaching yoga, working with a personal training client, hosting a meeting or event for the Network for Empowering Women Entrepreneurs, supporting my daughter through a mental health crisis, facilitating a Vision Weekend retreat, coaching authors to write and publish their transformational books, writing my own books, teaching people how to build and grow a conscious business, hosting a writing retreat on the beach in the Bahamas, or facilitating a Groove Dance experience in Puerto Rico.

The throughline was that I created sacred containers and spaces where people felt safe to share their truth, reveal their long-held secrets, free themselves from past pain, and step into the fullness of who they are with confidence, clarity, and courage.

See? The dots are all connected, through the lens of safety. As I more deeply embark on my own journey of feeling safe—now that I have the awareness that this is the great work of my life—I encourage you to reflect on your life. If experiences appear to be disjointed, there just may be a deeper gift for you to unwrap beneath the surface. It may not be easy when the awareness comes, but I assure you, it's well worth it.

Christine Kloser is the CEO of Get Your Book Done, LLC, Capucia Publishing, LLC, and Love Wraps, LLC. She's a *USA Today* and *Wall Street Journal* best-selling author whose company has published more than 650 transformational authors around the world. She continues to facilitate life-changing events and retreats for women and is the forthcoming author of *Feeling Safe: How to Make Peace with Your Past and Allow Yourself to Thrive*. Learn more and connect at: www.christinekloser.com

CHAPTER 2

Changing My Perspective

Denise Allen

It was 6:00 a.m. afterwards, when I woke from a deep sleep, thinking about them—the young mother who asked what to do about surgery for her infant, my daughter's friend who tripped and fell down the unexpected step leading to our house, the child who could barely read in second grade and acted out in class, and my nephew's daughter who had glasses at three because her eye started to turn in. I was thinking of those people and thousands more who see differently and don't know it, who misunderstand the problem, or who accept the status quo.

My thoughts turned back to that energy healing conference where I met a new author, Wendi Jensen, selling her self-published book. I envied her because she had done what I dreamed of doing: she had written a book designed to help people in a big way. The book was entitled, *The Healing Questions Guide: Relevant Questions to Ask the Mind to Activate Healing in the Body* (2013). I asked her if I could look at the questions she suggested to heal my particular concern, and she agreed. And I found *nothing*. There was no question specific to *strabismus*, *eye turn*, or even *amblyopia*. In a book of nearly 500 pages, there was nothing. I looked at her in disbelief. She had included six and a half pages that listed every other possible malady of the eyes, but there were only general questions to address my concerns: eye problems, right eye, left eye.

"The left eye represents your view of yourself or what is happening to you," she wrote in her book. I was stuck in the messy in-between, and I explained to her that I had done nearly two years of vision therapy at that point—some sixty-eight sessions to be exact—and had gotten nowhere. Like most people, she had never heard of vision therapy but thought it sounded like a great idea. She kindly suggested maybe I should face my reality and write a book about my journey to acceptance.

I protested vehemently. My deepest desire was to be just like my idol, Dr. Susan Barry, writer of the vision therapy essential, *Fixing My Gaze: A Scientist's Journey into Seeing in Three Dimensions* (Basic Books 2009). I wanted to inspire people with my story. I wanted to raise awareness of the problem and let people who suffer with similar conditions know they are not alone and there is help. It had felt so do-able at the start. I was the same age as she was (forty-eight) when I found vision therapy and began my work, but my brain was not cooperating.

Discouraged, I wrote a handful of posts on my website about how well vision therapy had worked for my daughter and some general informational posts. Then, I let things slide. Time passed and my developmental optometrist contacted me. He had trained in a new technique called *syntonics* (optometric phototherapy) and wanted me to try it. He warned me at the onset that he had been specifically instructed not to use it on his most difficult patients, but he was offering it to me anyway. He knew I was willing to try anything to avoid surgery. I applied myself to the endeavor and again experienced *nothing*.

Periodic evaluations were part of the process, and at the next evaluation a few weeks later, Dr. Davies indicated that there didn't seem to be any other alternative than to undergo surgery. He knew from our previous discussions that my goal was not simply a cosmetic fix, but he was hopeful surgery could be the key element in my healing.

It was not the first time we had discussed the possibility of surgery. I had been resistant from the very start. My brother had three surgeries as a child, two as an infant and one when he was seven and I was nine. His eyes had been mostly aligned for many years but, like mine, were starting to wander more as he aged. I had heard horror stories about how much more difficult vision therapy was when people attempted it after having surgery. And, there were the botched surgeries to consider. And the expense.

I decided to read Sue Barry's book again. My understanding was different because I had undergone so much vision therapy of my own. As I read, one sentence jumped out at me, and I haven't been able to find that spot since. It was like a message from heaven guiding my next step. She said that vision therapy works when the eyes are properly aligned. I reflected on Sue's eyes, which were already aligned by surgery when she was a child. I thought to myself, *This is the missing piece, and it's time to do it.*

I had work to do. My doctor referred me to a surgeon in our area he had collaborated with in the past. I waited for my first appointment, was evaluated, and was told it looked like I was a good candidate. However, they wanted to make sure. I asked a lot of questions and felt confident in the process and in the surgeon. They indicated that the new equipment they were receiving was designed to check how my eyes were likely to function after the surgery. I knew that I had put the building blocks in place with vision therapy, but they did not. So, I waited, wore the crazy prisms they attached to my glasses, and prayed.

The big day, March 23, 2017, arrived, and my mom took me to the hospital for the surgery. The receptionist and nurses were kind and effusive in their praise of the surgeon. My nerves started to settle. *Everything will be okay*. My mom took one last photo of me looking my absolute worst right before the surgery. Everything done with the prisms up to that point was designed to let the surgeon know how much correction was needed for my eyes to want to stay straight afterwards. Basically, the surgery would release the tension in my eyes, positioning them comfortably so they could easily work together. It was a *turning point* in so many senses of the word. I had not been able to release that tension on my own, and I had finally surrendered.

The surgery was on a Thursday, and by Monday I was back at work. My eyes were red, but since I couldn't wear my contacts yet, it wasn't noticeable behind my glasses. I took only one pain pill and didn't like the way I felt afterwards so I discontinued use. I had a homeopathic remedy, arnica, that helped greatly after the surgery. One week after surgery, at my follow-up visit, my surgeon was amazed at how quickly I was recovering. I went right back to vision therapy, and it was like magic. Suddenly, I could do the exercises we had been working on for so long! And my eyes looked good too.

I started receiving compliments, I looked people in the eye a lot more, and my confidence started to soar. Best of all, I started seeing in depth. Those with 3D vision can't understand what it is like to shift to this new way of seeing. Even now I marvel.

One spectacular experience from that time stands out. After the surgery, I decided to start a new activity with my mini-me daughter. She had already graduated from vision therapy, and I wanted to create an excuse to encourage her continued vision development as well. There was a dollar theater close by that periodically showed 3D movies, and we decided to see all the 3D movies as they became available. On our way home from one of those movies, it began to snow heavily. Before fixing my gaze, I would have been worried, but this snowfall was simply magic. We marveled together at how the snow came toward us into the windshield and surrounded us on all sides.

The world is so beautiful, and now, I can more fully appreciate that fact!

Whenever I catch something that's thrown at me, or something that is falling, I am amazed that my hand knows where to move. I make a conscious decision to park my car in that tight spot, because that phobia is deep set, and I navigate it well. The little things that are different are really the big things.

Whether you are dealing with vision issues or another health concern, the answer may seem out of reach. Maybe you have tried everything you could find, or the remedies seem too expensive or difficult. Vision therapy didn't work for me either—until it did. Be open to new inspiration or creative solutions. Most of all, persevere, because the destination is worth it.

Your journey is your own, and I am here to reassure you that solutions are available and encourage you every step of the way.

Denise Allen found vision therapy in 2011 and graduated to her new life in 2017. She is the mother to six children, two who also needed vision therapy. She created the *Healing Our Sight* podcast to support others on their vision journey. A graduate of George Washington University with a master's degree in music, Denise teaches piano and sells insurance when she's not sharing on Facebook strabismus support groups. Connect with Denise at healingmysight@yahoo.com.

CHAPTER 3

From Shutdown to Full Bloom

Karen Collier Arbel

I had always trusted my intuition and listened to my heart in figuring out my next steps. I sought out experiences to support my own emergence into better versions of myself, understanding that to be alive is to be dynamic and evolving. Whenever life presented that proverbial bump in the road, I did whatever it took to resolve any situation troubling me. I used challenges to stretch myself and to choose new ways of thinking about my life. There were times when I heard that still quiet voice within and knew immediately what was mine to do, while at other times I ignored it if it wasn't what I wanted to hear until, in the end, events compelled me to listen.

One such bump in the road was a major car accident. I was blessed to have survived. While in the hospital, I changed the trajectory of my life by deciding to relinquish my hard-earned place in graduate school for clinical psychology in order to start a family. I was passionate about becoming a mom after having put it off for years.

I gave my utmost while raising my two sons, but then the time was ripe again for me to launch my own career. At that very moment, my older son, who had already been living independently, shared he had been experiencing symptoms for a long time. He hadn't taken them seriously until they had become pronounced to the point of disrupting his life.

After an in-depth examination, the doctor called. I could tell from his serious tone that I should brace myself. I heard him say, "Paranoid schizophrenia." A suffocating silence ensued, and I stopped breathing for a few seconds. I became so quiet that I could hear a vast emptiness inside. I barely heard the doctor's perfunctory instructions. I hung up the phone and just sat alone in deafening silence.

My mind began swirling in disbelief: *How can this be? Hadn't he been accepted to the gifted program in high school? Hasn't he displayed talent not only athletically and socially, but also academically? Hasn't he? Hadn't he?"* I was in shock and taken totally out of my game.

I knew he would require my full-time care for a long while. Once again, life had presented one of those big bumps in the road totally unexpectedly, putting all else on hold. I was stopped dead in my tracks as all my memories of my son's growing-up years suddenly demanded reframing.

Up to that point in my life, I had shared my voice with the world, inspiring by example and giving support. In that moment, I made up my mind that it was over for me and whatever dreams I might hold for my own life. I chose to help my son put his best foot forward and wasted no time in self-pity or tears of victimization. I immediately moved into fourth gear to do whatever would help him.

I was finished investing in myself, finished striving in accordance with my true ability. I took on a whole new story about my life. I stopped nurturing myself, caring about myself, thinking about living my purpose, and evolving into my best version. I simply stopped.

I put everything I had into healing my son, leaving no stone unturned in seeking out-of-the-box solutions while pursuing traditional treatments. I was no stranger to my son's diagnosis as I had studied psychology and grown up among physicians and mental health professionals. I knew only too well the reality my son was facing. I was determined to find alternative solutions to buttress his success in life as much as possible.

After a few years of living in shutdown mode, I became a shadow of my former self. I gained weight, stopped socializing, and had little motivation to create a career beyond my 9–5 job. Though I helped my son very much, I noticed it was becoming increasingly difficult to do so. While considering the conundrum of how to take my son to the next level, I realized that I couldn't. I had stopped my own growth and didn't have the stamina. I didn't recognize myself anymore. I had become worried, anxious, and exhausted. Everything seemed so futile.

I had refused to continue blooming when my own son's self-actualization was obstructed. I couldn't bear the thought of moving forward while he still couldn't progress in accordance with his true potential. I felt guilty even thinking about self-actualization.

One miniscule ray of light was that I had maintained certain practices. I still meditated—mostly out of pure habit—because I felt more energy as a result, and I needed all the energy I could muster. I also had kept singing with my choirs and walking and playing with my dog every day. So, even though I was shut down, I still had tiny glimpses of a wider perspective.

During one of these glimpses, I had an epiphany: If I wasn't going to nurture my own self, be loving to myself, and invest in myself, then I was going to seriously limit my own ability to help my son. This was so awful a prospect that it jolted me out of living in the shadows.

Little by little, I returned to self-care, improved my nutrition, exercised regularly, meditated daily, and wrote. I further understood the deeper truth that playing small doesn't help anyone. I understood that shining my light is what would most illuminate the way for my son, my family, friends, and community.

In becoming the best version of ourselves, we give others permission to do the same.

I suddenly realized that it was actually selfish *not* to give my brightest light to the world. I understood better than ever before that our times of trouble are a God-given opportunity to shine our light as fully as possible. Actually, we are each encoded for just that: to bloom to our fullest potential, just like the acorn is encoded to become an oak tree. To give my best to the world wasn't just a nice thing to do; my sense of responsibility for my own life was aroused to a much greater extent for its potential positive impact on others.

I would not shirk this responsibility. This was my turning point, my transformation. My old passion to help heal others took on a whole new dimension in light of my own healing in the face of my son's trauma. I invested in a Life Coaching certification, and things suddenly transformed 180 degrees. My newfound joy, excited anticipation, gratitude, humility, and connectedness to my higher self inspired others. My vibration at home rose to a whole new level, and again there was joy, fun, laughter, hope, and inspiration for my son to put his best foot forward.

My sons had travelled to Italy two summers in a row with their dad. My older son said how peaceful he felt there and how much he wanted to live there. Though I had read that it is not good for people who have his diagnosis to move to another country, I knew my son would rise to the challenge. Once again, I listened to my own intuition and decided to try. We moved to Rome during one of the quarantines of the COVID crisis. Ironically, this was a significant phase of his healing journey that I had taken the courage to make happen despite the difficulties, believing that supporting him to stretch himself would help him. I was right.

I also found a doctor who understood the finer nuances of my son's case, and this understanding enabled a more positive outcome of his treatment protocol. Now, after two and a half years in Rome, my son will be moving to his own apartment and working on his own virtual project to generate income. He has been learning Italian, and next week he will begin working with a personal trainer to get into shape. He is on his own path of self-actualization and shining his own light ever more brightly.

As I awaken with the sunrise in Rome, I have noticed that the gray and blue hues of the Fall sunrises differ from the hot pinks and yellows of Summer. Each day and season reveal their gifts, all equally beautiful but unique in their own way—all contributing to the whole fabric of life. There is no judgement in nature and no holding back because of age or stage of life.

If you continually aspire to actualize your dreams, no matter the season or circumstances, you can experience the greatest truth and beauty of never-ending self-actualization. You can be at once fully animated and at peace, knowing that you have strived for your best in life and have helped others in the process.

Karen Collier Arbel has an eclectic background founded on spiritual and family values. She loves animals, singing, meditation, exercise, and sharing wisdom for the empowerment of others. After growing up a perfectionist and facing her son's heartbreaking health situation, she came out of a shutdown by embracing life's imperfections and learning to be a better person for it. She has a BA in Psychology and a Life Coach certification. Connect with Karen at: karenfullybloom@gmail.com

CHAPTER 4

The Diagnosis Misled

Diana Bacon

W*hy is my tongue numb? Man, this hill is steep.* These thoughts kept me worried as I huffed and puffed up the hill. *Am I the only one having a tough time trucking up the hill? The others don't seem the least bit tired. Aah, it feels good to sit and relax and chat about work as we order lunch.* Back at the office, I could barely function, and I still didn't feel right. *Maybe it's the heat or stress?* I felt swollen, puffy, and lethargic, not my usual energetic self.

Have you ever believed something wasn't right but didn't listen?

My scheduled trip to Atlanta was canceled due to 9/11. Americans were fearful and grieving, and only a few Americans were willing to fly. I was nervous about flying but was willing to take the risk for some much-needed R&R. So, on September 30, I boarded a flight to begin my two-week vacation with a few of my friends in Atlanta. I told my friend, who was traveling with me, I was stressed and needed a vacation.

We arrived in Atlanta on a clear summer day, and I remember the violet-colored Jacaranda trees in full bloom everywhere; it was simply stunning. It felt nice to relax and enjoy the scenery and particularly comforting to be with my lifelong friends. In the mornings, we hiked. With every step I took, I felt the warm air and enjoyed the vast rolling open green spaces and houses without fences, which made everything seem even grander. I was happy to be there, away from all my stress. As I looked up at the bright blue sky, I gave thanks, but I was still having trouble keeping up with everyone. I felt fatigued and exhausted for no apparent reason, even after a good night's sleep. I started to feel uneasy, wondering if something was really wrong with me.

Back home, I made an appointment with my doctor, who referred me to a neurologist. Over the next several months, I endured many tests with many different doctors:

- Magnetic resonance imaging (MRI)
- Spinal fluid examination
- Computed tomography (CT) scans
- Electroencephalography

They tested for everything, anything—or so I thought.

Finally, the results. Two different doctors confirmed I had *multiple sclerosis* (MS). Argh! I decided to keep this news private from my work while I processed my grief about having an incurable disease. An overwhelming feeling of sadness slowly rolled in as I made peace with what would be my new norm. I had just lived through the uncertainty of tests and questions before my diagnosis with MS.

The diagnosis made it easier for me to realize that there were certain things I could control and others that I couldn't. The terrorism strikes of September 11 were precisely the kind of event over which I had no control. I needed to remind myself that the uncontrollable could add to my stress, and I needed to try to remain calm during difficult times.

I endured daily injections, I had trouble walking, my legs were constantly numb, and I experienced pain somewhere in my body most of the time. With MS, the immune system mistakenly attacks the nerves. The damaged nerves then have trouble communicating with the brain. This condition can cause various symptoms, such as muscle weakness and fatigue (lack of energy). This all made sense to me, and I was relieved to finally have an explanation for what I was experiencing.

Four years after my diagnosis, I was still huffing and puffing up the hill, not really able to meet the daily challenges of my life. I was thirty pounds heavier. Living with MS was complicated, and I wanted to feel better.

So, I researched and discovered that yoga was a good exercise for MS. First, I ordered CDs and practiced at home, but I eventually found a nearby yoga studio and started practicing three times a week. I was quite happy with my increased strength and endurance. Finally, I was starting to feel like my old self and thankful my MS drug was working; I had no relapses or flare-ups. Amazing! What a relief!

During the spring, my yoga instructor announced she was conducting a twenty-one-day cleanse. Intrigued about removing toxins from my body and enhancing my immune system, I signed up. On this three-week journey, I experienced some powerful changes, inside and out. I was, at last, able to touch my toes. What a concept. My swollen, puffy, and lethargic body was back to normal, and my health began to stabilize.

I remember that one of my earlier blood tests revealed I had a high sedimentation rate of 150. A high sed rate is a sign of a disease that causes inflammation in the body. I found this interesting and wondered if my sed rate had dropped from the spring cleanse and vegan diet I had made part of my daily lifestyle. I went back for another blood test, and my sed rate had dropped to the normal range of 30. I was thrilled. How could this be? Did I have a food allergy? What did this mean? And what if my symptoms were all from some type of food allergy, and I didn't have MS? With all the tests the doctors had ordered, food allergy tests were not among them.

At this point, I had questions. I was tired of daily injecting a strange drug into my system at the cost of $2000 a month. Navigating the insurance maze was a nightmare. The kinds of hurdles I needed to jump through to receive the benefits my insurance company promised me in its policy were exhausting and stressful. Each month, I'd sit in my car during my lunch hour, reapplying for yet another program assistant scholarship.

What a life, right?

That was *not* how I wanted to spend my free time. I disliked traveling, hauling all my syringes and medication wherever I went. I was done. Finished. That night I sat in silence in my backyard and concluded I would stop taking my medication. I listened and heard within me: *It is time*. I was going to let the MS run its course. Then, I felt comfort knowing the disease would eventually take over my life. But hadn't it already, given my current lifestyle?

Will I have withdrawals from stopping the medication? This was the question I was going to ask my doctor.

The next morning I made an appointment with my neurologist. During the appointment, I asked if I would have withdrawals if I got off my medication. He said no, but although there is no cure for MS, he felt the disease-modifying medication was working and keeping me in remission.

Nonetheless, I stopped taking my medicine, and my sedimentation rate stayed at the average level. I couldn't help but think I wanted one last final review from a different doctor. I found a doctor at Stanford who specialized in MS to review all my X-rays, charts, and tests. Upon his review, he congratulated me for stopping my medicine and told me I had made the right decision: I did not have MS—I was misdiagnosed.

Hallelujah! What a shock—or a blessing. I was done for good. I was happy to close that chapter of my life and start a new journey.

Once I was out of my emotional fog, I realized how profound this experience was in my life. Moving forward, I put my health first, and

I've changed my overall lifestyle. Since changing what I eat and how I live, my body and mind are healthy, strong, and resilient. I've lost all the weight I gained while on my medicine. I've realized life is short, and at any given second, it can change for the better or worse, so I now embrace each day and live in the moment. I get up early every morning and meditate, then practice yoga. And I take full responsibility for my health and wellness. By listening to my intuition and believing in myself, I've become a self-reliant detective.

Are you huffing and puffing your way up the hills in your life?

I encourage you to adapt a new attitude. Fearlessness is how you will get through these types of hurdles. I recommend listening within and trusting in whatever outcome is meant to be. Review your life with honesty and compassion. Don't settle for the quick-fix drug that makes promises of automatic results. Be the person who bravely steps into the unknown and asks many questions. And don't stop until you experience peace and comfort within your heart of hearts.

You can heal yourself—listen from within for the answer.

Diana Bacon lives in the San Francisco Bay area. She's been a graphic designer and business marketing professional most of her career. She has degrees from the University of Santa Cruz and Notre Dame de Namur. When she isn't writing, she enjoys museums, yoga, hiking, discovering places off-the-beaten-path, and travel sketching. Connect with Diana at: thediagnosismisled@gmail.com

CHAPTER 5

When Times Get Tough: Stay Open and Listen

Yvonne Berenguer

There I was—sitting in the king-sized recliner my ex was letting me keep—curled up, staring blankly at the half-emptied living room. I could hear the sounds of the moving truck fading in the distance. I was left with nothing but the quiet hum of the refrigerator and the sounds of cars passing outside my once idyllic dream house. The shock of it all had not quite settled in.

That morning, I passively watched as he and his buddy packed up boxes and furniture that once held the story of the life we built. And in the moment, I felt powerless to say anything. *Say something!* I thought. But what could I say? This is what he wanted. Suddenly I experienced a brisk reminder about why it ended, and I realized that I needed to let this happen, needed to let go.

For a good couple of hours I sat there—balled up in that chair with a trusty box of tissues by my side. I was numb, unable to feel anything. But then the shock started to wane, and the waves of emotion I had managed to shut down during the morning rolled in. They rose in brief spurts as that was all I could handle. First came the feeling of anguish, and with that, the tears followed. Then came the feelings of deep pain and heartache, and with them, the tears transformed into sobbing. Next (allowing my body some reprieve) came calmness—perhaps with a surrendering or acceptance of my situation. These moments were welcome and allowed me just enough space to notice that I hadn't eaten a thing or that I needed to let the cat inside or out.

As the days and weeks went by, the cycle ebbed and flowed both in frequency and intensity. I allowed myself the space to feel the anguish and pain and to accept things as they were—as opposed to shutting things down. I gave my tears grace, asking their forgiveness for keeping them restrained for so long. There was no shame in this situation. I would tell myself (a particularly tough reconciliation since I come from an Asian upbringing): *No, I will not don the brave face and pretend that everything is all right, because it's not!* I chose to let things unfold and to take steps to honor what needed healing.

Once decided, I engaged on a path of self-reflection. For me, that meant immersing myself in a plethora of self-help psychology books and webinars—everything from understanding midlife crises to singlehood, from happiness to authenticity, from secular to spiritual sources. Of particular use to me was the body of work from Pema Chodron, an American woman who became a Buddhist monk following her second divorce. Her story resonated for me. She began the quest within upon her second divorce too. Like her, I found myself asking: *How did I get here? What was I doing (or not doing) that helped create this situation?* and *How do I move through this?*

I started journaling, almost religiously. Writing, after all, had always been the outlet for my voice as the pages would always lend me a willing ear. And in my reflection, I took inventory:

- Who am I?
- What's missing in my life?
- What's gone (or no longer needed)?
- What's left of me?

And more importantly I asked: Who do I want to be? How do I want to show up in life now? Figuring out the answers to these questions made me realize something: post-divorce is a lot like adolescence. It requires developing a new identity.

In developing this new identity, I needed to revisit the path that had brought me there. I had to connect to the pain associated with who I had become, understand the rationale for it, and figure out just who I wanted to be at that moment. I had to do a lot of soul searching about how I functioned in my relationships, especially the intimate ones. I had to acknowledge that I have a shadow side to myself—one that is not very kind to my partners—that is selfish, capable of doing hurtful things in order to feel in control of my life. I needed to shine a light on this part of myself that I didn't like if I was ever going to create a life that felt more genuine and authentic—more loving.

I'm older now, or maybe just plain *old* (lol). If you had asked back then if I ever thought I'd be twice divorced, go through single-motherhood again, and then embark on a path of personal self-growth and transformation, I would have answered, "Hell no!" That's nowhere near how I imagined my life would be at midlife. Yet, here I am, sharing with you what I've learned thus far about surviving divorce and embracing my journey for what it is.

I believe it's how we make sense of or how we think about our traumatic experiences that shapes what happens next for us. *The mind is a powerful force, but the heart is the carrier of true wisdom.* Too often we listen to our thoughts when what is needed is heart advice.

Oftentimes, it's difficult to fathom why things are happening as they are. It's so easy to feel victimized by the universe, thinking: *I didn't deserve this! I've been a good person in life, so why is this happening to me?* or *It's all their fault! This shouldn't be happening to me!*

But what I've learned through all the moments of loss is this: Whenever I had to face situations that caused me the most fear, heartache, or disappointment—where pain was the most profound—those were the events where the greatest learning happened, where the greatest personal transformation occurred for me.

From the many teachers I've had along the way since my divorce, I discovered that things were not being done *to me* as if it were a punishment of sorts. But rather, things were happening for my benefit, so that I might step back, reflect, and explore how to grow from the experience. I learned to ask: How might I learn from this?

So what exactly have I learned thus far? It's this:

- Find what feeds your soul. Be okay with taking some risks and planting new seeds, and then nurture what you want to see in your life because what you feed grows.
- Learn to find joy in the mundane or little moments in life, and you will gain a greater appreciation for what you've been given.
- Accept that things will never go as planned because the real adventure lies in the unknown.

But most of all: Stay open and attuned to your heart. Or as a wise fortune cookie once told me, "Make decisions from the heart, and let the mind figure out the rest."

Holding space for you and sending you loving kindness always.

○

Yvonne Berenguer is a writer, wellness coach, and college educator. As a natural progression of her journey, she discovered the joys of journaling and poetry. This eventually led to her writing more content in the arenas of personal healing and well-being. At present, she is working on the completion of her first book. She is also a contributing writer to *Elephant Journal* and is the author of the *Stay Open and Listen* blog. Connect with Yvonne at: www.yvonneberenguer.com

CHAPTER 6

Finding Home

Tara Chatterton

A message gently worked its way into my awareness, a knowing that changed the course of my life. This moment shook me awake as I realized it was time to change. I was being shown what needed to be healed, but by the time I caught wind of it, my wounds were buried so deep that it would take a lifetime to heal them.

Belonging is something that one feels when they are at home in the world, but I never felt like I fit in my life. Every aspect of my surroundings revealed the discord I felt inside. I tried to be what others wanted and often agreed to things that just about destroyed me.

I was in over my head, keeping my business afloat during the 2008 recession. The stress of running multiple businesses between my husband and I began to show the cracks in our foundation. Our house was always under construction, despite my husband's determination to do the work himself. He inevitably lost interest but refused to work on a solution. After years of pleading, I became desperate to find a place to land, take up root, and create a sacred space for myself, but he was unable to empathize with the ways in which I was drowning.

My childhood home wasn't much different. Growing up poor showed itself through disorder and neglected home repairs. There was a heaviness there that settled within me like quicksand, making it hard to leave, but left me wanting to escape.

I witnessed and experienced things that taught me lessons no child should ever have to learn. Silence became the veil that separated me from the outside world. The lack of guidance and occasional predator kept me lost in a sea of undefined boundaries, a sea that filled my lungs and welled inside me like an abandonment I could not purge.

There were no reassuring words or comforting gestures to affirm that I was safe or worthy of protection. All I could do was attempt to shield myself, hoping others wouldn't see through my exterior, inevitably revealing what I couldn't live with on the inside. So I internalized the neglect I felt to mean something about myself that was never true, but my child self did the best she could to protect me and be the parent when others failed to.

Being highly sensitive and empathic, I felt the inadequacies of others as if they were my own. When others projected their fears onto me, I became paralyzed from the amplification of terror in my body, causing me to unconsciously insulate from this interference I felt in others. I couldn't cut through the noise and speak up for myself.

It was as if I was a target for such things and was heavily bullied for years. In addition to the chaotic environment I was raised in, mirroring what others couldn't stand to see in themselves made it difficult for me to connect with the world around me. I became an open landscape in which the fears of others set up camp when I wasn't looking.

Emotions are energy, and I was vulnerable to energy, even beyond this realm. I often struggled to wake from nightmares that held me down. Like static to a clear channel, my fears summoned distortions within my reality, playing with my sense of control. As if under a spell, their influence animated my worst fears. The importance of being embodied, so as not to allow these *hauntings*, was foreign to me.

Eventually, I began to decipher the invisible realm that overlays this one, in which painful emotions are an open door for lost souls.

As I grew older, I was unaware of what was stirring within me. I thought moving away would allow my life to be different. It wasn't until much later that the past began to repeat itself. Parts of my life began to crash down around me. I felt trapped in my marriage, but didn't feel I was *enough* without him. My home life was chaotic, and I experienced debilitating health issues that stole my livelihood and led to the loss of my retail business, eventually causing me to hit rock bottom.

Only then did I reach a turning point, during which I was able to touch the core part of myself, buried beneath this extremely deep mother wound. The transmission from mother to child imprinted upon me in such a way that her fears became my own. The depressive state she was in cloaked me like a blanket I had never been without. She was depleted after having five kids and caring for my older brother who had meningitis. My parents were headed for divorce, and she needed to break free from years of abiding by the rules that had been set out for her. Raising her kids reminded her of the life she wanted to escape, so she found her joy in going back to work instead.

Living in her shadow often felt like a punishment, as if I wasn't allowed to live my own life. It distorted nearly every experience I had. Reclaiming myself meant defining myself apart from the past and realigning with what felt true. Yet, I didn't know, or even trust, who I was without my experience.

Suddenly, the disrepair of my home became glaringly apparent, as I went through the motions of trying to figure out how to repair my life. The countless abandoned projects that we couldn't keep up with seemed endless. It never became a home I felt proud of. It lacked my essence entirely. I fell into waiting for life to begin, while tolerating a marriage that didn't consider my needs and expected me to settle for the unacceptable. The things that brought me joy were lost. I yearned for social gatherings and decorating artful spaces, yet found myself over-explaining the construction and oddities to the occasional guest until I avoided having company altogether.

I slowly began to see myself apart from my experience. The heaviness I felt in my body wasn't my own, and the empty shell of a home I lived in didn't represent me. Seeing the bigger picture eventually pushed me to bring out the part of myself I'd been hiding all these years. As I came to recognize the shadow aspects of myself and others, I learned to perceive these distortions as an overlay that hides one's light.

We think we know who we are, but so much of what we don't like about ourselves has been imposed upon us, handed down through generational wounding that allowed a thread of darkness to weave its way into our story. I became well versed at pulling out that thread.

Every time I empathized with another's needs over my own, I abandoned myself and returned to the familiar thread of darkness that entangled me. It was no mistake that those around me were often consumed by their own demons. It took years to learn how to protect myself and to stand up to those who overshadowed me.

Navigating this alone was isolating. My husband was unavailable and couldn't comprehend my personal journey. We were like oil and water, yet two sides of the same coin—mirroring each other's scars perfectly. I knew I wasn't honoring myself by staying, but with my health the way it was, I feared I couldn't make it on my own. I needed time to heal, but staying meant living under a perspective that kept me answering to past versions of myself I no longer identified with.

In order for me to heal, I had to start putting myself first. This decision alone has allowed for my healing to take place because it defies the past and breaks the cycle of settling in the face of fear. If all I can do is come home to myself each day, I am doing my life's work, simply by acknowledging who I'm becoming.

Growing up with complex trauma altered the way I live my life. Experiencing ongoing stress from the time I was born made regulating my emotions and nervous system challenging, causing isolation and dissociative behaviors, such as normalizing unrealistic expectations of myself, seeking approval from others, and berating myself for failing. Through observation, I learned to notice when I was reacting from a trauma response and began to heal those parts of myself. It took years to understand that healing does not involve removing the trigger, but rather, having the awareness to respond differently so that I can redirect the pathway.

Every day, your life is a choice, with all its complexity and contrast. With each eclipse, you can still choose to live on purpose. Many things happen beyond your control, and you can either resist the challenge or glean the lesson that it offers. This is the opportunity you have in every moment. When you learn to react less and observe more, you will see that everything is happening to bring you back home to yourself.

Tara Chatterton is a transformational coach, facilitator of healing, and writer. She's soon to publish her first book that embodies the principles she uses in her work. Tara developed her own healing method for integrating the subconscious shadow parts of the self to assist her clients in reprogramming past emotional experiences. Tara lives in the Pacific Northwest. She is a lover of dogs, beautiful spaces, nature, and family. Connect with Tara at: tarachatterton.com

CHAPTER 7

The Little Bucket of Nails

Gloria DeVoil

Stuck. That's all I could see. *There's nowhere to go, nowhere to run*, was my first thought after concluding, *What do I do now?*

Momma, Daddy, and my four older siblings were completing the work to be done to our recently purchased home, requiring inner, non-structural work inside and outside completion or a *shell home*.

Momma, the visionary, had purchased a small plot of land in a coastal town, and Daddy, a laborer, landed a job with a construction firm and made friends quickly. Momma decided to find work on her own to become more productive. She felt that with her nursing career and training, she could get a job to pay her bills and contribute to the family. She thought she could be crafty, work on the newly constructed house, and make it her own style.

My two elder brothers, Ben and Elijah, and two elder sisters, Anna and Sara, always had everything all figured out. They would go to school, then do their extracurriculars, and then take up small jobs from time to time. My eldest brother Ben loved walking our two dogs and cutting grass for the neighbors. He made good money and learned to deal with animals and look after them. He jokingly told me that he enjoyed doing so because that's how he learned to look after me when Momma and Daddy were away at work, but my elder sister Sara wouldn't let him take over. Sara was a babysitter, so she always argued that I would be much safer staying with her at home. The four siblings had already done anything I could think about doing.

I, on the other hand, had nothing going on. I would sit and wait for someone to ask me for help because they all were concerned that I was too young for anything of great responsibility or difficulty. I didn't find being the youngest as fun as everyone assumed. What is the fun if people do everything for you because they feel you can't handle it? I wanted to do things. I would go to everyone in the house asking for work, and they would tell me I was too young to do anything meaningful.

Why? Because I was just a seven-year-old whom everyone treated as a princess. Picking up on this princess-like attitude towards me would cause me to sometimes snap and ask, "Don't princesses have any work at all?" I was sure that even if princesses had some work, there must be a reason why they were so pretty, rich, and wanted by almost everyone. I wasn't sure if I wanted to be a princess, but I sure knew one thing: if I did, I wanted to be a helpful princess. If there was such a thing.

One morning as I woke up and walked down to our makeshift dining area, I noticed a crowd of people dressed up in work gear; I walked up to Daddy and pulled at his pants lightly to get his attention. "What are these people here for, Daddy?" I inquired.

Daddy bent down, smiled, and hugged me tightly. "These people will help us with the house and make it look more pretty like your Momma wants. Those folks in orange vests with wires in their hands are here to help set up wiring and electricity. The ones with those goggles and helmets are the carpenters, and the ones in the bathroom down the hall are the plumbers."

I took a moment to study them and take a mental picture. I then looked at Daddy and asked, "What does a carpenter do?"

"Well, sweetie, the carpenter makes things out of wood, like furniture, doors, and cabinets. They also install sheetrock petitions, walls, and other things."

"What about the plumbers?" I asked again.

"Plumbers set up taps, toilets, bathtubs, and all the pipes," he said as he put me down.

"Then what about electricians?" I asked, looking up at him.

"They help us with the lights, fans, and all the other things that would need the power to work. They set up the switches and lighting for us to use."

I took a moment to contemplate, sitting down for a minute, then jumping back up again and again and again. I couldn't stay still. Grandma would have said, "You're acting like you have ants in your pants." I just wanted to do something. After all, it seemed like everyone else had been given significant responsibilities, but what about me? I kept peering out to see if there was something I could do.

But if I asked, I knew they would look at me like I was crazy and repeat the same answer, while patting me on my head. "No honey, sit and play with your dolly, or color in your coloring book."

Finally, I got my nerve up, thinking this might be the perfect time to ask Daddy another question. "Do you think any of them will let me help?"

Daddy pursed his lips for a second, sighed, and replied, "Ugh. How about you ask them?"

I jumped up excitedly as I was about to run towards them to ask for help when Momma stopped me. "Not so fast! You need to have breakfast before you go and get some work done," Momma said as she picked me up and put me on the chair at the dining table.

I pouted as I sat down and waited for my breakfast. Soon breakfast was right before me, and I scarfed it all down, excited at the thought of finally having something to do.

I rushed to the men dressed for work and moved from one person to another, offering them my help. Some men said no or told me they would call for me if they needed something. A little discouraged, but still more determined than ever, I approached one lady carpenter. I mustered up what courage I had left, walked up to her, and asked, "Is there anything I could help you with?" I asked nicely.

The lady, having noticed everyone else said no, looked down at me and smiled. It felt like I may be finally getting something to do. It appeared at first that she would say no, but then I saw this little shiny bucket of nails positioned near where she was working, just sitting there as if it was waiting just for me. It seemed to pull me towards it, and I immediately made a connection with it. I begged her to let me carry it for her.

Without hesitation, she asked, "Do you think you could handle this little bucket of nails?"

I was over the moon. I beamed at her nodding my head excitedly. "Yes! Yes, I can. Thank you!" I exclaimed gratefully.

She warmly smiled at me again as she handed me the little bucket and allowed me to carry it. Feeling full of confidence and pride, I took the bucket in my hand and followed her around the house as she installed sheetrock walls and fixtures all over the house. I was thrilled to finally have something meaningful to do and to join in working with everyone else. I felt like a big girl building the house. While my older brothers and sisters had more important and more significant tasks to help with, I was finally happy that I was able to do something important also.

I swung my little bucket around, hip-hopping and trailing behind the carpenter lady with my little bucket in hand. I imagined this little bucket of nails was taking me into mystical worlds, believing that anything and everything is possible. I treated those nails like something precious, like Christmas ornaments or diamonds all piled up in the bucket as I followed the carpenter lady around the house.

I finally felt I could do something and maybe be a useful princess.

Sometimes, we may feel out of place in a busy world that is constantly changing and moving around us. Even with this challenge, we may still find that there is something within us, an internal work, that drives us to seek out our own *carpenter*. The carpenter is observing and waiting to help us along the way to get *unstuck* and find our own bucket of nails to complete the inner work in the non-structural areas of our lives.

Gloria DeVoil is a retired certified project housing manager and a transformational leader with a deep passion for personal growth and development. During her career, she served in the public sector for over twenty-five years, working with diverse individuals and families. Gloria has a knack for writing and is driven to mentor and inspire individuals to help them realize their full potential. Her transformational style is marked by her ability to inspire and empower others to embrace challenges and pursue their passions. Gloria can be reached at: scionchangers@gmail.com

CHAPTER 8

Always at Choice

Larry Freeborg

In 1979, I learned a valuable lesson about how fragile life is. That year, within ten months of a fun visit with my wife and four children to Disney World in Florida in March, my young thirty-nine-year-old wife died from *acute myeloblastic leukemia* (AML). She died the day after Christmas, and I became a widower with children ranging in ages from nine to sixteen.

The country was in trouble economically. Within two weeks of my wife's funeral, I was told to terminate ten people in my marketing department. Within five months, my job in staff marketing was eliminated, and I was told to find another job within the company I'd worked over eighteen years for. That same day, the president of the company froze all personnel requisitions.

Here was my situation: I was forty-one years old, no wife, no money, four children to raise without a partner, many losses, no job, and unemployment was at 10–12 percent. I was scared.

One day, all the stress and loss combined, and I broke down in tears in the office. I left early to see if my parents could take care of my kids. I wanted to escape on a solo trip to sort out my life. Within a few days, I would learn when my loss and stress points were tallied that I was off the chart, and no one was surprised I was asking for help. Except me!

My father suggested I contact the company and see if they might be able to help. I had access to the company psychiatrist, so I called him. He made time to see me that afternoon. After I explained my situation, he asked if I'd be willing to place myself in the psych ward of a local hospital that afternoon.

I said, "You bet!"

Fortunately, I had learned how to use professional consultants in my business life, so I didn't see any stigma in asking for help in my personal life. I was relieved I was going to get some help.

My new beginning started in the psych ward in June of 1980 with a *situational depression* diagnosis. There was a good reason no one was surprised to see me. Stress experts say that if you have 100 loss/stress points there's a 50 percent chance something physically will go amiss in your body. At 300 loss/stress points, there's an 80 percent chance something will go. When they tallied my loss points for six months, I exceeded 500 loss/stress points.

Life changed for me with Shirley's death. The sun still came out every day, but my life would no longer be the same. That phase of my life, being married, living with Shirley, and raising our children together, was over.

A big realization for me in my life journey is that life is short. For some, life is shorter than others. Unfortunately there are no do-overs. *This is it!* If life throws us some curve balls or if we've made a bad decision, we need to accept what's happened and move on. If we've lost a loved one, we need to accept what's happened and move on. I'm not saying we can get by without grieving. If we're truly loving and compassionate people, we will grieve whenever we've lost someone or something we really care about. My point is that our own lifetime is limited, and life keeps going on while we're grieving.

I don't believe we're responsible for the things that happen to us outside of our control, like hurricanes, tsunamis, death of a mate, loss of a relationship, or diseases like COVID, but I do believe we are accountable and responsible for what we create in our lives, and we are always *at choice* regarding how we handle situations.

I speak about my life before forty and after forty. The gift my wife gave me, with her life, was the opportunity to learn that I am always at choice, and I can choose to live joyfully and in gratitude versus in sadness and depression.

My turning point came from an experience in the psych ward, where I learned I was always at choice.

The occupational therapy selected for me was learning how to cook again. I cooked for six months when I was ten and my mother was in the hospital with Guillain-Barré syndrome (GBS), a disorder in which one's immune system attacks their nerves. In high school, I earned money as a fry cook and later managed and cooked at the Glacier National Park coffee shop. I did well with hamburgers, cheeseburgers, eggs, pancakes, and roast beef, but it had been years since I'd cooked a full meal.

The condition of the occupational therapy lesson was that I had to follow a recipe and *do it right*.

I decided to bake a chicken and ordered all the materials in. I took the materials into my cooking room, and after a couple of hours of chopping celery and onions, liver, and heart, and boiling them to make the broth for the dressing, I found myself getting angrier and angrier, *with a French knife in my hand*. I was concerned I might hurt myself or someone else.

I asked to see someone, and they sent me to my room to wait for a consulting nurse.

The nurse came into my room and said cheerily, "Hello Larry, I hear you're having a bit of a struggle. What's happening?"

I responded angrily, "I've just spent two hours working on preparing this GD chicken for baking, and that's how I'm going to live the rest of my life. Cooking for my kids!"

She said, "Well Larry, it sounds to me like you're going to have to grow up."

I blew up and started sharing information to establish that I was grown up: "I'm forty-one years old, have four kids, been a leader of Toastmasters, Kiwanis, and AFS, and I'm a marketing manager of a major Fortune 500 company."

She said, "What I'm trying to say is: *You're always at choice.*"

Again I angrily responded, "It's not a choice. I have to take care of my kids." My father had taken care of me, my brother, and my sister when my mother was in the hospital for six months. He was my model.

Patiently and respectfully, she began to offer alternatives: I could have my folks watch over my kids. I could send my kids to schools where they could stay in residence. I could split the kids up and have my relatives take care of them. I could send my kids to foster homes.

Finally, I said (to get her off my back), "All right, I choose to take care of my kids."

She said, "Good. Now you *can choose* how you're going to cook for your kids. You can cook for your kids. You can hire someone to cook for your kids. You can purchase prepared meals. You can hire someone to teach your kids how to cook."

And I got it! I was *at choice* regarding how I cared for my kids and how I cooked for my kids—and I was always at choice regarding how I looked at life's problems. I could need to, want to, have to, get to, choose to do something. If I *choose to* do something, I am in control versus being forced by *needing to*, *having to*, or *wanting to*. *Getting to* gives me the opportunity to feel grateful for the opportunity, but the most positive, forwarding statement for me is *choosing to*.

I wish I could say I only had to learn this lesson once, but I've been reminded throughout my life that I'm always *at choice* regarding my life decisions. I've had many other turning points in my life and have benefited from a lot of good help and assistance along the way, but this lesson that I'm *always at choice* laid a foundation.

Today, because of the choices I've made, I have a lovely relationship with my second wife Dodie (we've been together for thirty years). I'm happy to report that all four of my children have graduated from the college of their choice and are all living satisfying and fulfilling lives, with normal life-learning opportunities.

After leaving the company where I worked over eighteen years, I joined another Fortune 500 company for five years. I went on to create my own strategic planning facilitation business called Business Development Specialists. My business is now called Stepping Through the Gate, and my focus is helping individuals with major loss or setbacks in their life gain clarity regarding their situation, accept it, and move on to capitalize on their new life possibilities.

No matter how bad things can seem, we're *always at choice* regarding the action we take. Rather than looking at our lives as something we *need to do* or *have to* do, we're much more successful and happy if we *choose to* do the task.

Larry Freeborg was forty years old when his wife died from acute myeoblastic leukemia on the day after Christmas. He became a widower with four young children, ranging from nine to sixteen years of age. Larry started his life over in a recession, as a widower with four children, with no job, no money, and no wife/partner to help him raise his children. Now, Larry works to help individuals live *at choice* after major life setbacks, such as he experienced. Learn more at steppingthroughthegate.com

CHAPTER 9

Retired, Old, and Accepting Who I Am

Marilyn Garrett

Except for the summer of my 1959 wedding and my daughter's first baby year nineteen years later, I have been working since high school. My first job was at Woolworth where I switched between the candy counter, fish and turtle care, and working at the cash register with never a dull moment. My next high school job was as a secretary and assembler for a small electrical company.

Always, during many college and advanced degrees, I worked—mail room clerk, dining room waitress, and even as a drill press operator, trying every day to increase my final piece count, which impressed the bosses—though my coworkers were not so happy. Later, I enjoyed successful careers as a public and school librarian, university instructor, and Realtor. Most recently, I worked with family in an advertising business while also having my own business providing ad signs along a 300 foot walkway to Crabby Joes restaurant in Daytona where guests can view the ocean between floorboards while dining.

Granted, I should have retired long ago. Presently eighty-four, I've been encouraged for years to quit and enjoy retirement. That's where it gets tricky. I actually enjoyed every job I've had during all these years. But, did I keep working because it defines me? Perhaps I wouldn't like the absence of requirements? I don't think so, because I have many things I want to do. I'm never bored, and I have a travel and hobby bucket list.

However, these questions became irrelevant last September when I suddenly became unemployed. My family sold its business, and hurricane Ian wiped out Crabby Joes. Suddenly I became retired—and old.

Easy to see why that's a dramatic turning point, right? It's the *old* part that's especially scary. I was sick a lot last year: a long, bad cold in February, COVID all of August, and upper respiratory and flu most of November. I struggle to feel like my old self again, to have energy and gumption. No longer will it be possible to assume I'll always get better and back to normal.

It's time to get serious about that bucket list before moderately strenuous excursions become overwhelming. Fortunately, my twenty-three-year-old granddaughter is happy to cruise with me—three times since December! We have so much fun as amazingly compatible travel buddies. Cruising is an easy way to see the world when you're old.

As a lifelong learner, I've always followed this motto: *Half of knowledge is knowing where to find it*. Got a question? Go to library or bookstore for a stack of books and seek answers. That's how in 1978, I chose to have natural child birth in Orlando's brand new and only birthing room. That's how I discovered meditation and natural ways to treat extreme stress. That's how I wisely decided to ensure retirement income by owning inflation-proof rental property and holding on for dear life through good times and bad.

You can see where I'm going—I got a stack of books from Amazon about growing old.

Many of the books on the topic discussed *How to age gracefully*. Apparently, I needed to better check the definition of *graceful* if I wanted to understand what was ahead. I remember pieces and phrases, such as *polite and pleasant* and *smooth and controlled*. More relevant were the ideas of *positive yet quiet confidence* and acting with certain characteristics, such as *charm and poise*. Graceful people are apparently *not pushy,* and they don't throw tantrums or play emotional games. I wonder: Is society worried about what people growing old will do if they're not graceful? I think I'll just not focus on graceful. I think I'd rather live exuberantly.

There's also lots of advice about staying active, eating well, getting enough rest, exercising, staying involved with family and community, and making final plans such as living wills, actual wills, and funeral preferences. I can see that's all useful. Perhaps, I can put off my real-life unfinished business by completing all these tasks and following good advice.

See how quietly I snuck that in? Did you notice the mention of unfinished business? There's no way to discuss my past life without the *Journal of ChristIAm*. I wrote about this life-changing turning point experience in the 2013 second wave of Christine Kloser's *Pebbles in the Pond* transformation anthology series, which is available on Amazon. That night, January 9, 1989, was the first time I came out of meditation and found a message on the tablet beside me that I had written as dictation from God's voice within. I had no memory of the process, but the message was beautiful and just what I needed to hear to help heal what was happening.

I could not wait to hear more, lots more, for I was sure that the speaker I heard and transcribed was indeed "Spirit God, your co-creator, ever present with thee, and within All That Is." Even more astounding was the message just six days later in which God proclaimed that my name is *ChristIam*.

ChristIAm—pronounced Christ I Am. I was told over time in my transcriptions that the name speaks the truth of who we *all* are: "I

Am the presence of God as Soul and Spirit manifesting in human form to experience the joy of Spirit truth." When you say this name, you affirm not only who I am but who you are also.

Say it: *Christ I Am*. "You are the Christ, as are all of my Beloved. You, Soul, and I, Spirit, are One, and the Presence of Spirit is within You, and Is You at every moment, giving only love, and fulfilling the desires of Soul" (*Journal of ChristIAm* 2/12/89).

I thought: *But God, am I really to call myself ChristIAm? To whom? How will people react? And how does this affect what I will do on a daily basis?*

I disclosed to a few family and friends what was happening—and the name. There was quiet concern, no enthusiasm, and little that could be called support. Word spread just enough for my daughter to lose a friend. But I listened, and scribed, and bravely self-published the *Journal of ChristIAm* in 1991, containing all messages verbatim from January 9 through September 18—131 pages, including an index and a sample page of a transcribed message.

There was no marketing since this was pre-internet and pre-Amazon. My how times have changed in just thirty years! Any knowledge of the *Journal* was limited to the local spiritual book store where I led meditation and guided imagery events. Perhaps the results of my disclosure would be different today, due to the popular attention given Neale Donald Walsch, whose first *Conversations with God* was in 1992. But I'm not sure about that. It is not shocking anymore to learn of people who have personal experiences with God.

The biggest challenge for me to accept has been the name ChristIAm. Even though it is clearly meant to refer to each of us, all of us, calling myself that name seems unfathomable. Could you call yourself ChristIAm? We are each a unit of God, the living Christ, One with God. "I go with thee, I am within thee, I and thee are One Beloved, and in your knowingness, you speak with Me that truth—I AM, I AM, I AM!" "See ONLY divinity, for that is all there is ChristIAm" (*Journal of ChristIAm*).

It has been thirty-four years since that first message. The Soul part of me would like to say that my lifelong journey has been to share my experience, the *Journal* messages, and the name ChristIAm in a life dedicated to Spirit. The truth, however, is that I haven't been able to call myself the truth of our Being, ChristIAm, as I feared the judgment of others. Sure, I have excuses. I was a single parent and also had a dependent parent; I had no choice but to focus on providing for family. I can check that one off now—no one needs my help anymore.

What indeed would you do on a daily basis as ChristIAm? It's easy to judge my journey and the reluctance to respond to the voice of God with full acceptance of the challenges. Will you accept the name for yourself? I think we all judge ourselves pretty harshly most of the time. But I've been told that the journey is the goal, and that there is no judgment, ever. There is also no hurry; we will all reach the goal. I leave you with words from the *Journal of ChristIAm:* "Slip and fall if you must, but do so knowing Who You Are—ChristIAm."

I come full circle, back to sudden retirement that comes with freedom to choose again and again what I want to accomplish from the bucket list to experience a life well lived as I age exuberantly, maybe even gracefully. Obviously this chapter about transformational moments is on that list. And, right here, I commit to sharing incredible messages in a new thirty-fifth anniversary celebration volume of the *Journal of ChristIAm*.

Namaste.

Octogenarian **Marilyn Garrett** enjoyed several careers: as a young adult librarian, a high school and college teacher, a Realtor, and in media marketing. During meditation in 1989, while seeking self-help for debilitating stress, Marilyn was stunned by the unexpected experience of transcribing messages from God, leading to her book, *Journal of ChristIam.* In these messages, she learned that we are all spiritual beings with the same ability to listen to the Divine voice within.

CHAPTER 10

The Card Deck of Life

Dondrea Beth Garrison

In April 2001, about four hours into my shift as an inpatient physical therapist, a patient passed out and fell on me. The pain was immediate, and I knew I would be sent home, but I told myself it was just a bad sprain. I assumed that with rest, ice, and PT, I would be back at work in no time.

It didn't go as I planned. After fourteen weeks of extensive treatments, I was still unable to return to work. I was told I had permanent damage to joints in my lower spine and pelvis with disc damage at two levels. A few doctors told me I would never work again. I refused to believe them. I knew that bodies didn't read books. I had treated too many patients who had defied the odds, and I knew in my heart that I just needed more time.

However, there I sat, one day after my thirty-eighth birthday, reading the letter that was terminating my employment and essentially ending my ten-year PT career. I couldn't continue as a physical therapist based on the current medical assessments. I had been forced to activate my personal long-term disability policy, and I simply didn't know how to play this card.

I kept asking myself, *What do I do now?* I was in a full-blown identity crisis. *Who am I if I can't wrestle and run with my beloved nieces and nephews?* I felt most alive being outdoors and active. *Who am I without the hiking and long-distance bike races? Who am if I can't do the work I love?* I started working when I was twelve. Working is how I gained independence from a challenging childhood, and until that moment, I hadn't realized that my career had become an identity from which all other aspects of my life branched off. I lay in bed at night, asking over and over, *What do I do now? Who am I without this job and these roles?*

The journey to that answer and to where I am today started when I was six years old. Have you heard the expression, *There are no wasted experiences, just opportunities for lessons and growth?* Well, when life is filling your hand with challenge card after challenge card, this statement can feel insulting, demeaning, or just demoralizing.

For most of my childhood, I felt like no matter where I was, the card decks were stacked against me. I couldn't control the cards, much less understand the rules of the game. I experienced a series of abandonments; time in a children's home; emotional, psychological, and sexual abuse; and a period of serious suicidal consideration. I survived because of the unknowing intervention—at several key points in my life—of people who showed me that love, acceptance, and encouragement could exist in life. A lot of those people were authors I never met, but whose words and stories gave me hope. Along with these authors were key family members and three teachers who always believed in me and my potential.

The one deck of cards in my life that had never let me down was education. It had clear rules and I excelled there. It was the one place I thought I could control the cards. With this in mind, one month after my eighteenth birthday, I boarded a plane for the first time and flew almost 600 miles away to the college of my choice, excited to finally start creating my own card deck of life.

It started off pretty good—but yeah, you guessed it—choosing my own cards wasn't as easy as I thought. I could choose them, but the results still seemed far outside my control, and those challenging cards still kept coming. Plus, there was the additional frustration of realizing it wasn't easy to discard the effects of those childhood cards. My life kept bouncing from one path to another, each card leading to a series of choices that moved me from starting college as a pre-med student to graduating with a computer science degree and knowing on the day I was graduating that I wanted to become a physical therapist. That's a story for another chapter.

I fell back on the one thing that had always helped me: I was a voracious reader who loved to learn. In one of the many books I read not long after I graduated, I came across a discussion about how we seem to only question why bad things happen, but never question why good things happen. This insight resonated strongly with me, and I started to be more conscious of the *gift* cards in my life. Soon, an even more pivotal gift landed on my path, also via a book. I discovered Jack Canfield's $E + R = O$ equation: the event (E) + my response (R) = the outcome (O) (jackcanfield.com). Up until that point, I had pretty much been living the belief that the event created the outcome, and my attempts to control the events hadn't been working well.

I fully embraced these new concepts, and armed with this change in my belief perspective, I started taking ownership of my choices and responses. Lo and behold! My life path evened out. I realized that my responses to positive events (gift cards) were just as important as my responses to the challenging events, in terms of outcomes. I was learning to own my part in the process.

Six years after my first degree, I completed my second and began my career as a physical therapist. I continued to actively pursue my own healing through the reading of many books, as well as a few years of therapy. I slowly learned to trust again through the gifts of love and acceptance from key family members and friendships. I developed a new belief that no matter what cards came my way, there were two things I could always control: how I defined the cards and how I played them. And this was working well right up until that 2001 termination letter and the end of my PT career.

What ultimately pulled me out of my place of despair was spending time really looking at those metaphorical cards in my hand. I spent time going over my life's gift and challenge cards. Reviewing my childhood and life experiences from this distant perspective showed me how much of my strength, perseverance, stubbornness, empathy, and will to live came from the very things that had almost broken me. Some of my greatest challenges had turned out to also be my greatest gifts.

I realized that everything in my life was a card: my personality traits, the people in my life, all experiences and interactions. In hindsight, these cards are neither good or bad. For each card, one side has challenges associated with it and the other side has gifts. When playing those cards, I can choose to discard those that no longer serve me and keep the lessons I learned. And for those tough cards I can't discard, I put them in a hold pile and only let them in my hand when I have to. But no matter what, I control how I define the cards and how I choose to play them. I call this my *Card Deck of Life* philosophy.

So where am I now? Six weeks after that termination letter, I found out that a new physician assistant (PA) program had started in Albuquerque, New Mexico, which was ninety minutes from where I lived at that time. I had all the prerequisites. I applied, interviewed, and was accepted, and three and a half years later, I graduated and started my next career as a PA. I am now in my twentieth year of that career! As for my injury, time has notably improved my abilities, and I have learned to listen and let my body tell me what I can and can't do each day.

Why was that Physician Assistant program opportunity so pivotal?

Five years into my PT career, I questioned my decision to not be a doctor. I finished the classes I needed for med school but decided not to go because of my age. Five years later, those classes met the prerequisites needed for the program.

Now, for that expression: *There are no wasted experiences, just opportunities for lessons and growth.* Frequently, it requires time passing for us to fully see both sides of the cards we are dealt. However, we can remind ourselves regularly to take a breath and give gratitude for the gift cards in our life, and for those new cards life keeps dealing. We can ask, *What are the challenges and gifts of this card? What are the options for response?*

How do you view the cards you are dealt in this life? What challenges are also opportunities for you to grow and branch off into a new adventure? What gifts have you gained from your life challenges?

Remember, your power always lies in the impact your response has on any outcomes. If your first response doesn't go as planned, choose another. I encourage you to explore the stories you are telling yourself about some of the cards you've been dealt and ask yourself which stories are serving you and which are limiting you. They are your hand of cards, so don't let anyone else play them. And above all else, remember the key word—play.

We each get one life; create your joy in the playing of your hand of cards.

Dondrea Beth Garrison is an aspiring author and speaker. She is a passionate, active advocate for expanding peoples' knowledge, understanding, and motivation on their health journey. As a medical provider of twenty-nine years, Dondrea is driven by her curiosity around the forces that move us towards or away from our best health. Dondrea holds Bachelor of Science degrees in Computer Science and Physical Therapy as well as a Master of Science degree in Physician Assistant Studies. Contact Dondrea via linkedin.com/in/dondreabgarrison or email her at: carddeckoflife@gmail.com

CHAPTER 11

When The Fat Man Sang

Donna Goldman

You know that saying: *It ain't over 'til the fat lady sings*? I'm sure many of you are saying, "Of course, D." Well, I was in my forties when I learned that the masses equate this phrase with baseball games. I, on the other hand, heard this barked out at me over the decades while preparing a classic wooden yacht to round the last mark of a race, invariably a downwind leg when your position in the race is likely to change because too much is going on to take the sails down and get the spinnaker pole and sheets in place to raise and fly the spinnaker.

I'm using this metaphor to explain the moment I knew my deep-hearted connection to working in the international rock 'n' roll touring industry cord was cut. As I walked out of Gate D, the backstage, load-in tunnel of Giant's Stadium, circa 1996, to relay the most recent weather forecast to the production manager—who was holed away in an undisclosed location outside of the stadium—about the impending thunderstorm threatening this ginormous entertainment spectacle, "The Three Tenors at Giant Stadium." It wasn't the *fat lady* that sang, it was the largest of the Three Tenors, Luciano Pavarroti, who was singing for me.

Later that night, like a lightning bolt that threatened the show, it struck me when Mr. Pavarotti belted out his final aria. I got the message. The cord and heartfelt attachment I had to this world was finally cut. This moment and realization was two years in the making.

Here's the scenario of the *aha!* moment that created a new pathway in my mind two years prior to this night. On the morning following the last show of Peter Gabriel's WOMAD festival in the Golden Gate Park Polo Fields, September 1994, I savored a breakfast of two toasted, scavenged heels of an ordinary loaf of whole-wheat bread with warm butter and spun honey and a steaming cup of Earl Grey tea on my friend's sun deck on a crystal clear fall morning in the Oakland Hills.

I heard these words from deep within me: *When you're on the road, your every whim is catered to, and I'm not just talking about food here. Anything you need and want is at the ready for you.* Yet, I never felt satiated by any of this. I realized then that the energy or life force we bring to preparing food, or any undertaking for that matter, is vital to our mindful well-being. Where your intention goes, energy flows.

With the "Three Tenors" circus tent stakes pulled up and the dozens of semis rolling on to their next gig, I was laid up on my futon couch without the prospect of a job. I had another late night tirade, yelling at a television celebrity chef, "Not everybody has an eighty thousand-dollar prop filled kitchen with a Fry-a-lator, a standing mixer, a Cuisinart, ramekins, or a dozen mixing bowls!" Nobody should feel intimidated watching a cooking show. This is when I declared I should have a cooking show that would be the antithesis of all this. Hence, the seed for *Recipe$ 4 $urvival, Utilitarian Cooking and Much More . . .* was planted.

A friend insisted I start writing daily and gave me Natalie Goldberg's *Writing Down the Bones: Freeing the Writer Within* (Shambala

2005). I took to the practice like a bee in search of honey—naturally. I coupled this with reading Julia Cameron's, *The Artist's Way,* in which I came upon this statement, *"When we are awakened to the nature of our unique gift and if it may be of help to others, this is the emergence of true Buddha nature"* (Penguin Random House 1992). Finding this made me realize that my cooking abilities, which I took for granted, just might be my unique gift, and if I presented cooking techniques simply, I could probably be a help to many, many people.

With my mind finally stimulated, I began writing a proposal for my utilitarian cooking show concept to pitch to the Food Network. At around this same time, I had a friend over for dinner. I served a broccoli-cheddar quiche, a pot of green tea, and chunks of fresh pineapple for dessert. Once we were settled in, I mentioned all this to her.

She bellowed out, "Wait a minute. You're laboring to write your concept proposal because you want a job at the Food Network? Are you kidding, D? You're a fabulous cook, hysterically funny—never mind with a voice that will snag anybody's attention—and you've got a video camera. Get on with it, girl. You'll own the idea!"

I had to laugh because I hadn't thought of this. The following day, I called my friend Michael, who was directing infomercials, to see if he would impart any advice on me. He was so into the idea he agreed to come by the following Sunday to get me going. He showed up with a tripod and a 200-watt clip-on floodlight we clipped onto a shelf in my kitchen. The tripod was placed just over the threshold in the *living space* on a 45-degree angle that framed my kitchen perfectly. This, he said, would create *depth of field*.

Michael sputtered pointers at me as I worked in the kitchen, "Have all your ingredients and utensils out. Don't turn your back to the audience and remember—talk to the camera. That's your audience." And we were on. Michael hit the record button on the camera and proceeded to sit down and read the Sunday *New York Times*. The camera came with a remote so I could stop the recording, clean up, and get right back to it. This experience was so empowering. I could do it all. All on my own.

When Michael was leaving he said, "D, watch the tape. I know you're not going to like it much but keep at it. I think you're on to something here." Michael left me with the tripod and the light. That was November 15, 1996.

Unfortunately but naturally, with Michael's departure and the equipment folded up and tucked away, I was back on the futon. About three weeks later, a friend from my artist collective invited a few of us to his apartment to watch his show premier a Manhattan's public access channel. As I watched this truly avant-garde musician, videographer, and puppet maker's show, I thought to myself, *This public access platform might be perfect for me to test and hone my skills for my utilitarian cooking show.*

That night—actually in the wee hours of the morning—I set the equipment up and got to it. I taped myself making whatever, in sweats with my eyeglasses on. That same day, I trudged in a snowstorm to the Manhattan Neighborhood Network office to see about getting a show on there too.

I filled the one page application out without even removing my winter headgear. Name, address, and phone number(s). Have you ever produced a show on public access: No. Type of show: I circled *cooking* from a list of categories from AIDS awareness to youth counseling. Title of the show: *Recipe$ 4 $urvival.* Brief description: Utilitarian cooking and much more. It would be a weekly show. I don't remember answering about a preferred time slot.

Eight weeks later, I opened an oversized yellow envelope that had my thirteen-week schedule and videotape labels that looked something like this:

0484	#1/13	Recipes For Survival
4/03	09:30 p.m.	17

Translated, this read: My first show would air April 3, a Thursday night, at 9:30 p.m. on channel 17. This was prime time and a bullseye for this channel because this was the dead half-hour following *Seinfeld on NBC, channel 4.* Channel 16 was A&E, 18 was the Discovery Channel, 19 and 20, VH1 and MTV.

It didn't take long before I was recognized at art openings and once by a taxi driver. He said he knew me because of my voice.

I share this story with the hope that I've inspired you to trust in generating calm and reflective times for yourself for these times are when you'll hear your intuition. Your unique talents are Source energy to be shared for the benefit of others. You are a masterpiece—a piece of the Master.

We're meant to *Live It Up!*

Donna Goldman is an author, narrator, and storyteller. She continues to develop and host various spinoff projects from the *Recipes 4 Survival, Utilitarian Cooking and Much More . . .* platform. An abridged version of her memoir is available on Audible and Kindle. The R4S podcast focuses on recipes and lifestyle tips to help alleviate food packaging waste. She continues to keep her voice and messages relevant about caring for our planet. Visit: www.recipes4survival.com

CHAPTER 12

Shooting Stars

Raven (Becky) Goodgain

At the age of thirty-three, as a mother of two young children, I received the devastating news that my mother had been diagnosed with lung cancer just after celebrating her fifty-third birthday. My heart sank as I struggled to come to terms with this reality. My upbringing had been far from easy, with my single mother often overwhelmed and checked out, leaving me as the oldest to take on the role of caretaker at a young age. My childhood was marked by abuse, bullying, and a sense of isolation even from those closest to me. By the age of sixteen, I was living with my grandmother and overwhelmed by the challenges of life.

At that moment, I decided I was better off by myself, so I ran away from home.

Despite facing daily challenges, I managed to push through and support myself to finish high school and enter college.

It wasn't until I was in college that my fiancé insisted that I work on mending my relationship with my mother. Honestly, that was the last thing on my mind, but I listened to his advice. It took years of counseling, but eventually, our relationship began to heal. By the time I became a mother myself, the relationship between my mother and I had blossomed into something beautiful, and we became closer than ever before. Finally, she had become the loving and supportive mother I had always longed for.

Unfortunately, her body succumbed to the cancer, and she passed away at the young age of fifty-four. My whole world shattered. I couldn't fathom why this was happening to me, given all the hardships I had already endured in my life. Losing my mother, who had become my best friend, left me wondering: *How am I supposed to move on?*

After her passing, I spiraled into a deep depression that not only took a toll on me, but also on those around me who depended on me to be okay. It took almost a month for me to return to work, and even then, I felt so empty inside. It was as though I was a lifeless body walking around.

In the weeks after returning to work, I was overwhelmed by anger, sadness, and depression. Day in and day out, all I could do was try to figure out how to move forward with this enormous hole in my heart.

Desperate for a sense of closeness to my mother, I began asking for signs that she was still with me, even if only in spirit. I was seeking any comfort I could find in order to find a way to heal my heartache and be able to function.

Then, something remarkable began to happen. My mother started sending me signs to let me know she was with me.

One of the most incredible signs that she often sends is shooting stars. Yes, you read that right—shooting stars. Living in the city, I rarely get the opportunity to see stars, let alone shooting stars. It's a rare and magical occurrence.

For days, weeks, and months after her passing, I would be driving home after work, crying and missing her dearly. As I rounded the bend before my house, without fail, a shooting star would streak across the night sky. This was her way of showing me that she was still with me, even though she was no longer physically present.

This went on for about a year. Then as I started to heal and grow stronger, these signs became less and less frequent. It was as if I no longer needed them to get through each day.

Although it has been thirteen years since she passed, I continue to sense my mother's presence, even though she is no longer here physically. Whenever I miss her or need to feel her presence, I look up at the night sky and ask her to send me a shooting star. She never disappoints me. I have seen more shooting stars since my mother's passing than most people do in a lifetime, and some may never see one at all.

During a recent writing retreat, I contemplated writing about my mother in this book. For about a week and a half before the retreat, I could sense her presence. I even caught whiffs of her favorite perfume from time to time.

Approaching the final evening of my stay at this beautiful one-bedroom Chalet for my writing retreat, I indulged in an incredible bath before settling into a comfortable gazing chair beside a sliding glass window. As I looked up into the vast, star-filled sky, I took a deep breath and whispered, "Mom, if you're here, you know what to do." Almost instantly, the biggest, massive shooting star I had ever seen streaked across the sky, causing my heart to sink with emotion. I knew it was her; she had never let me down before.

But being the skeptic that I am, I challenged her, "Okay, Mom, I know it's you, but send me another shooting star." Not even a minute later, another shooting star blazed across the sky, leaving me utterly amazed and grateful to have not only seen one but two shooting stars back-to-back in one night.

Overwhelmed with emotions, I sat there with tears flooding my eyes and falling down my cheeks, and then a third shooting star flew by—all in less than five minutes. Wow! It was truly indescribable.

I was reminded once again, that even after all these years, my mother was still there for me, even if she wasn't physically here in the present.

Losing a loved one can be an extremely challenging experience, primarily because we believe that death signifies finality and that once someone has departed, they are gone forever. However, this perception is simply not true. We are essentially *spiritual beings* living a physical existence in this world. Even when we pass away, our physical body may cease to exist, but our spirit lives on.

Understanding this fundamental truth, after all these years, grants me the courage and optimism to keep my chin up and continue moving forward. It comforts me to know that I can always call upon my mother whenever I need her and that she's never left my side.

Have you ever experienced the pain of losing a loved one? Are you aware that it's possible to call upon them for signs or support to let you know that they're still with you? While this may sound implausible or even unreal, it's true. The spiritual realm is beyond what our conscious minds can fully comprehend, and it's not something irrational. If you believe in angels, a higher power, or a god, you already understand that there are unforeseen forces at work in our lives. Asking for signs from your loved ones is simply an extension of that belief.

If you can accept the possibility of their presence, you are one step closer to seeing their connection.

In my experience, the best way to ask for a sign from your loved one is to begin by requesting something that they cherished during their physical life. For instance, what was their favorite animal, song, or catchphrase?

The signs often begin subtly, like seeing a bird or hearing a familiar tune. As you begin to recognize these signs as connections to your loved ones, they tend to become more frequent and pronounced, providing you with a sense of comfort and reassurance that they are still with you in spirit. Frequently, I express my appreciation and then request the continuation of signs whenever they happen to manifest. This simple step conveys to our dear loved ones that we have acknowledged their message and are open to receiving more.

Initially, my connection with my mother began with bluebirds, as they were her favorite, and she had the most beautiful striking blue eyes. As soon as I spotted them, I felt it was her way of communicating, and seeing them made me feel as though she was with me. Nowadays, shooting stars catch my attention, and her favorite song plays randomly on unexpected radio stations. Moreover, I still occasionally catch a whiff of her favorite perfume without any explanation whatsoever.

Do you have a way of perceiving the absence of someone dear to you that has passed on?

Would you consider requesting signs from them if you had the faith and conviction that they would appear?

The initial step is to have faith and be open to signs, regardless of how they show up.

Raven (Becky) Goodgain finds immense joy from music, traveling, cooking, being outdoors, and her three children. Her strong spiritual roots have played a vital role in helping her surmount painful challenges throughout her life. Despite being shy and timid in her early years, she has since evolved into a daring adventurer with an unshakable *I can do it* mindset, enabling her to triumph over heart-wrenching obstacles and emerge victorious. Connect with Raven at: raven@speakyourtruthboldly.com

CHAPTER 13

From Stroke to Freedom

Maureen Harrop

It is under the greatest adversity that there exists the greatest potential for doing good, both for oneself and others.
—His Holiness, The Dalai Lama

A Stroke

It was 4:00 p.m. on Thursday, September 17, 2015. I arose from a nap. Suddenly, I was falling to the floor in slow motion. A strange sensation ensued. It felt like a zipper running down my spine. It didn't hurt; instead, it was debilitating. The left side of my body was completely paralyzed.

I was alone in the house and needed to reach the phone to call 911. Where was it? I crawled down the hall by pushing myself with my right leg. Terrified, I screamed out to Archangel Rafael, the healer, for help.

Eventually I found the phone. It was on the end table next to my chair. I was unable to rise up to retrieve it. Some part of my body wasn't working, so I waited and strategized.

Somehow, my brain was as clear as could be, operating on overdrive: I had to get help. I refused to die.

I looked up and saw a small pillow on the arm of my chair. Instinctively, I raised my right leg, pointed my toes, and gingerly lifted the pillow up and over to the table. I slowly moved the pillow toward the phone and used the pillow to push it onto the floor. Thankfully, it dropped on my right side.

I placed the phone on my chest and attempted several times to punch in 911. Finally, I was able to do so. The operator asked for my name and to describe the emergency. "I think I've had a stroke," I responded. I have no idea how I knew that.

Her name was Gloria. She dispatched the paramedics, who responded quickly, I'm sure, but it felt like hours to me. I was transported to the hospital where I learned I had experienced an *ischemic stroke*, a blood clot. Once inside the emergency room, I was relieved until the doctor who admitted me thought he was Don Rickles. He wasn't—trust me—and I didn't appreciate his fruitless attempt at humor one bit. The nurses, on the other hand, didn't take this situation lightly at all. They sprang into action. Their flurry of activity made me dizzier than I already was.

Since I didn't get a chance to thank them then, I now want to thank the all-female nursing staff of the 5:00 p.m. shift on that date at Flagstaff Medical Center. I was grateful to them then, and I am now for their kindness, expertise, speedy action, and compassion. I truly wouldn't have made it through if it hadn't been for them. *Thanks!*

Much later, I was transferred to a semi-private room, where I remained for one week. Then, I was off to a live-in acute rehab facility for another three weeks and then home to begin my neuro therapy. Being at home, with my kitty on my lap, was priceless.

Listen, staring death in the face changes you. How could it not? Read along, and you will see how it changed me.

A New Moon

One night, a dear friend drove up from Tucson to Phoenix to visit me in the acute rehab facility. I had been inside the facility since I was admitted—a dreary existence—so she decided to wheel me out into the dark, cool October night. Eventually, she stopped the wheelchair and turned it facing the moon, and said, "Look at that beautiful moon."

I did, and asked, "Beautiful moon? Really? It's all black," which was about the way I was feeling. She patiently explained that a New Moon signified new beginnings. In the moon's case, it was the turn toward becoming a Full Moon. In my case, it had a spiritual significance. It was my opportunity to begin new phase of my life. Specifically, I needed to choose how to proceed with that new beginning in my life, to chuck off all the old patterns and begin anew. That has led me into a self-awareness journey like no other.

She told me I had a choice of how I wanted to live from this point on. What did I want to change in my life? What were the things that no longer served my highest good? What would I learn from all this? It was my choice: A choice of self-destruction, pity, victimhood, and misery? Or a choice at beginning anew, finding new horizons to explore, new ways to improve myself, to learn, and to grow? I wondered what path I would choose.

Well, I certainly had a lot of time to think, and this new way of thinking and questioning about what I really wanted in life would lead me on a path like no other. It's been priceless, and I may never have moved in this direction had it not been for my stroke and my friend's generosity with her wisdom.

A Blog

Four years post-stroke, I got to work. I'd made my choice. I decided to combine three things that had impacted my life. I created a blog for stroke survivors and their caregivers. It was the blending of my father's analogy of having two hands—one hand to help ourselves and the other to help others—my friend's New Moon advice about choice, and my love of writing.

The blog was a gift, a game changer for me. It provided me with a vehicle to move out of myself and to help others cope with this life-changing disability and to give them hope. In turn, I helped myself. *Providing light that displaces the darkness* is the message I attempt to communicate in my blog.

We're all in this together—helping ourselves and helping each other.

One of the many benefits I've gained as a stroke survivor is being able to enjoy new friendships, work with empathetic and gifted therapists, and to meet other survivors so I know I'm not alone on this journey. And the biggest bonus is learning about and experiencing my spiritual side, facilitating the wholeness and depth I was missing.

I try to help my blog subscribers create a *toolkit for recovery*. I ask: *What are the things that sustain you, motivate you, inspire you in your life?* My personal toolkit includes such things as: good nutrition, moving my body in whatever way I can that day, laughing, reading, watching old movies, socializing with friends, listening to music, journal writing, dancing, and fun. What sustains, motivates, and inspires you?

If you've experience a setback, joining a support group is also a good idea. Support groups not only help you feel you're not alone, but they also provide some great ideas for coping and flourishing. An added bonus is forming relationships with people who may turn out to be lifelong friends. Spend some time now to create your own toolkit. You never know when you might need it. Being prepared never hurts.

My journey of choice happened to be creating a blog for stroke survivors, learning and growing in directions I never dreamed of:

- Meeting the most extraordinary stroke professionals who love their work

- Meeting other survivors and many other non-professionals
- Intensifying my current friendships and making new ones
- Experiencing a disability I'd never wish on anyone as gracefully as I can muster
- Learning gratitude for all the good—and even the bad and ugly
- Cultivating patience and forgiveness, which are currently works in progress
- Finding ways to work within my limits to help myself and others maneuver through daily tasks and emotions

Setbacks are crummy, for sure, but they're opportunities for us to grow and learn, not excuses to be miserable or victims of our circumstances.

If a medical event happens to you, use it as an opportunity to learn and grow. Use it to aspire to be like the Dalai Lama or someone you greatly admire. Why not? It's so much better than wallowing in self-pity, loneliness, and victimhood, but we've all been there. No one is perfect. The key is to allow yourself time for those difficult feelings so you may then choose to move on and become a better person

A Final Thought

You may be wondering why I chose the significance of the New Moon instead of my stroke as my turning point. It's because I feel my stroke was the turning point for the physical side of my body, but the New Moon experience was my spiritual turning point. The latter was much more profound, much deeper, and more life-sustaining. So, I'm much better off as a human being than I would've been had I not had a stroke.

I cannot close until I thank my incredible caregiver, my partner in life for these past twenty-six years, Jane. She certainly deserves the *Caregiver of the Year Award!*

My warmest wishes to you, one and all.

Maureen Harrop has a background in hospitality human resources and employee training, having been an executive in the resort industry. She has a MS degree in Early Childhood Education, which she translated into teaching pre-school and kindergarten while living in New York City, teaching college classes in Scottsdale, Arizona, and finally, as the owner of an employee training business for thirteen years. She now writes a blog for stroke survivors: www.strokerecoverysolutions.com

CHAPTER 14

To Human Be or Not to Human Be

Sue Henry

The root of the word courage is cor*—the Latin word for heart. In one of its earliest forms, the word courage meant "to speak one's mind by telling all one's heart."*
—Brené Brown

Our feet do so much more than walk us places. When we are on our way to meet a lover, they grow wings and float us on air. When we perceive danger, they spark fire and propel us to safety, and when we are unwell, they become heavier than lead and anchor us to earth's source for healing.

Walking towards the stage where I was about to perform, seeing it stretched out before me, wooden boards glinting, it felt as if I were wading upstream of a rushing river. The stage grew closer and all else dropped away, leaving only the drum of heart in my head and the journey of breath, tight in my gut. The same feet that carried me to the bathroom, the shops, and the dinner table now brought me face-to-face with the mic. Opening strains of guitar penetrated my core, and from the soles of my feet to the tips of my hair, sound welled within and flew through my lips and mouth. And I flew with it, free.

That is the first time I remember singing my heart out.

It is also the first time I remember feeling as if my world had fallen apart and nothing would ever be all right again.

I was six years old, and over the previous year, my enchanted life had been overcast with the looming shadow of my parents' divorce. It was only the three of us in the house, so if my parents became sorrowful ghosts, and our home a shelterless hollow, somehow it was up to me to bring them back to life—to light them back up—so we could all be okay again.

But try as I might, the ways which had previously engaged and connected with them no longer worked. They still loved me, but the shock of what was happening to them took so much of their focus I couldn't feel that love. I felt cast adrift, irrelevant, and fearfully alone.

That was the first time I remember feeling like this, but it wasn't the last time. I recognize now that I've responded this same way to changes in external realities at other times too. The only certainty we have in life is that it is transient, so whether at work, in relationship, or in health, we will at some time or another inevitably experience axis-tilting shifts in what we have come to know. Sometimes these shifts happen not just to us individually but on a global level.

The best I've personally learned to do when life takes an unexpected diversion is to let go of the need to try and force it back on track. If something I cannot control is causing me to suffer, I've learned there is a fraction of a moment in which I have a choice. I can either react to the turmoil I am feeling by trying to return things to how they were, or I can be present with my shifting feelings and open to hearing where these new circumstances want to lead me.

Whenever I choose to listen instead of acting out, I find suffering softens at its edges, and in time, there is yielding to a new reality, often one more expansive and creatively abundant than the previous one I had so wanted to hold on to.

That first time with my parents' divorce, I didn't realize what I was doing, but after playing out, playing up, and using any arsenal I had, at some point I let go of trying to make things go back to how they had been. One day the unravelling discord in our kitchen was just too much, and my feet and inner life propelled me away, up the stairs to the living room, and on to the next stage. My stage.

In the day, Lulu's version of the Isley brother's song "Shout" was flying high in the charts, and I loved *everything* about Lulu: her feistiness, her hair, her clothes, her voice. That voice! It shattered so many glass ceilings; impossible became possible when Lulu sang.

So with a toilet roll, a ping pong ball, and a piece of string, I made a microphone. I even drew little black dots on the ping pong ball for effect. Well, how else was the sound going to get in?

Then as I stepped off the living room rug onto the parquet floor, the real world dropped away. I reached for my mic, the record began to spin, and as I waited for the opening strains of guitar, nothing existed except unity: unity with music, with vitality, with an imaginary sea of faces so lit up with love no possible force could tear us asunder. I was on my stage and ready, ready to sing my heart out. Ready to sing my grief free.

Naturally it takes more than singing a song to release grief, and when the waves return, we must choose: do we surf against them or allow them to carry us back to shore? Can we be with what *is*, rather than what we wish it *was*—a human *being* rather than a human *doing*? In my experience, when things get dark and stuck, taking that moment to listen before acting guides me to resources I didn't know I had. In time, the next small step becomes clear, that step lights up the next, and a new unanticipated path opens up ahead.

Remembering to press pause is not easy, however. Our societal norms encourage us to live evermore outside of ourselves, losing the precious moments of now, grasping for an elusive future when we will *have* enough, *know* enough, *be* enough to really start living our lives. My favorite definition of this is from Carrie Fisher's book *Postcards from the Edge,* in which she quips, "Having a wonderful time. Wish I was here"(Simon & Schuster 2010).

After many years of trying to bend and shape life to how I think it should be and failing, I now find it easier to lean in to change than deal with the fallout of trying to resist it. Earth and nature have their own rhythms. We cannot force them to meet ours—nor should we try—but we can align our life to meet theirs.

It's always such a relief when I remember this. While in rhythm with the cycles of life as they happen, there is no reaching or yearning needed, no summit at which to arrive. There is simply a small step *yinwards* toward what is. A remembering of who in essence we already are. As a dear friend of mine once advised me, "Remember that you will forget. Oh, and don't forget to remember."

I've personally found channels, such as dance, nature, chanting, or study, help me recalibrate in this way, but there are many portals beyond the obvious ones, and—although each opening leads to a place where there is unity—each individual has their own unique way of getting there.

The opportunity could arise any moment in life. For some, it's in butsuma, synagogue, mosque, or church; for some it's when playing football, putting children to bed, hearing birdsong, or speaking to a neighbor. Each moment is a possible turning point.

Including. This. One.

On a more profound level, I have seen rifts between people—that for years seemed impossible to mend—find an unimaginably creative way to heal when deeper listening replaced finger pointing and preceded speaking.

"Know yourself," Socrates once declared when asked to sum up what all philosophical commandments could be reduced to. Over the years in my work as a coach, I've observed that each time someone is brave enough to search within, listen deeply, and—with their humane imperfection—bring heart to their words, they light up. This more than anything else is what inspires other people to truly listen to them.

When we light ourselves up, we shine the way for another, and together we turn some small corner of the world around. This is what it means to have a voice, and my hope is that when enough people use theirs and encourage or speak out for those who can't, we may see a beauty growing around us we can barely now imagine or even think possible.

Your feet do so much more than walk you places. And your voice does so much more than speak words. Both enable you to travel from where you are now to a future you have yet to create.

Your wisdom speaks in a quiet, clear voice—can you hear? It's asking you to bring your unique story of healing and harmony into that future.

Your courage speaks in a gently powerful voice. Take a moment now. Hear that? It's the voice that makes your heart sing a little, no matter what.

And your heart's voice. Oh! When that speaks, you'll know it. Your heart's voice is rooted and infinite, and it calls out your unspoken potential to live with loving respect for yourself, others, this planet, and life itself.

Your unlimited innate ability to fully, Human Be.

Pause. Listen. Now. Can you hear it?

Sue Henry is a performance coach, leadership mentor, and facilitator. Since 1993, she has been delivering her bespoke group programs and 1-2-1 sessions extensively across the private and public sector. Her clients include LSE, Google, Oxford University,

PRS for Music, LBS, Fierce Grace, and The BBC. Sue has had a daily mindfulness practice for over twenty years, sings jazz, and specializes in helping people reach their audience by freeing their most authentic and inspirational voice. www.suehenryvoice.com

CHAPTER 15

Pissed to Positive

Dr. Cecilia J. Howell-Canada

Here is a story of an atypical life overcoming atypical hurdles to have atypical experience in order to enjoy and realize the positivity within myself and the world around me.

My personal and professional journey has covered the United States, visiting locations that allowed me to experience cultures with atypical challenges. Along the way, I decided *why not* ignore negativity and make positive strides to have an exciting life with memorable experiences and enjoy the journey. Each journey has been unique with a common thread of simple positivity that was powerful when fully actualized.

I developed a mindset of mind-over-matter: how to get it done, finding what's needed to get it done, and then finally asking, *Why not do it?* This plethora of experiences led to opportunities that became my foundational building blocks as I remembered to not fall back into a negative mindset of *can't, won't, should've, would've, could've,* but to instead keep a *Why not?* mindset.

I was existing in two circles of life: one between the stages of death and dying and the other between the stages of shift to sail, not realizing how these circles overlapped. I was stuck in a stage of one cycle but didn't realize how it was affecting my progression in the other cycle. Due to an emotional event in my professional life, I found myself in the cycle of death and dying in which the stages of denial, anger, bargaining, depression, and acceptance were having a deep effect on me psychologically.

Movement in the cycle of my personal life was overcast by these stages in my professional life. As I came to understand what I was experiencing on a deeper level—going through this cycle of death and dying—I realized that each stage needed to be addressed so I could progress through the process and move on. I did not realize the mental, physical, as well as emotional ramifications this event had on my body, mind, and soul.

At first, I did not want to exit and experienced negativity, yet I progressed and grew into being positive. Once I realized I needed acceptance about my professional cycle, my life cycle could move on. When I realized I didn't have to be pissed anymore, the judgment was in my favor, and I could continue forward.

My struggles were characterized by doubt, causing self-limiting behaviors that led me to question my abilities and keep looking over my shoulder when providing services. Providing services without comprehending the internal impact of a negative mindset led to a standstill: I was not moving forward mentally, physically, or emotionally.

To peel the layers of my total being, I had to deep dive into my body, mind, and soul for determination, exploration, and evaluation. Once I realized the death-to-dying cycle was completed and I accepted it, I was able to move on. The judgment was then in my favor, and a pissed mindset was no longer welcome in my head space.

My heart and my mind had not been able to grasp: *Why not be happy? Why not be successful? Why not be all I can be?* Being pissed all the time was draining my energy, bringing me to the lowest level of my being. I had to look inside my mindset and examine the reason I kept asking *why* instead of *why not*. The internal impact of mental negativity—the *not being good enough* mindset—caused me to exist in limbo mentally, physically, and emotionally.

Why not have an attitude of gratitude? My attitude of non-gratitude segued into an attitude of gratitude with the understanding of the *why not* effect in my life. The *why not* moments unleashed experiences of growth through harnessing the positivity within, knowing the answer lies in looking beyond the circumstance and seeing the potentiality of any situation.

During a prelude to an early morning coaching session, I realized negativity and anabolic energy had crept into my life and overtaken my very being without me even being cognizant of the subversive activity. For me, the struggle was looking from the outside inward and moving forward in a positive direction, thus turning a negativity mindset into a positivity perspective.

Learning how to be, look, and feel more positive than pissed was the struggle, due, in part, to the negativity of family and friends. I made a decision to break out of the *poor me* mold, dig down deep, and realize that I had rich life experiences to capitalize on—the *why not* energy deep down within me—to pull me up and move me on.

Sift—shift—shed—shred—stretch—sail. I had covered up the smiles that got me through, covered up the adventurous nature to move on, covered up the *why not* and *who says I can't* attitude of non-gratitude. There came the shift of sifting what was in my life, shifting what was in my life, shedding what was in my life, shredding what was in my life, and sailing in a new direction. New choices abounded with new adventures, unexplained opportunities, and advantages from all around, creating a positive cloud wherever I went.

My mindset shifted as I went through the process of sifting, shedding, shredding, stretching, and then sailing to address and come to terms with the process that allowed me to get rid of the burden—the heavy-feeling cloud of negativity—that I had been carrying for so many years and reclaim that fun and exciting and adventurous person of long ago.

Once I had completed the journey inside of myself, I re-established the joy that gave me a sense of balance and re-defined my peace of mind. This major shift allowed me to have new choices with a positive vein running through them. This *Re-Re* factor is for whatever you need.

Realization leads to actualization. Through an evolution of my *Re-Re* factor actualization, I gained re-juvenation, re-birth, and re-defining. I am so much more positive than pissed. Re-alizing that no matter whose (friends, family, or job) poop falls on the path, it's going to stink; it just doesn't have to be mine.

Poop stinks. I choose to smell it or not to smell it. I don't have to be held down by my past because I can't go back; my present and my future lie ahead. I choose for my body, mind, and soul to be positive and purposeful. I have learned to communicate within myself to prepare myself to be viable and full of vitality.

Wisdom is available at all stages. Building on it leads to knowing what one can and cannot accomplish from within. I know now the journey has been an opportunity to understand myself, my journey, my work, my house, and my *why not*. My ongoing journey affords me the opportunity to identify the *pissed versus the positive* moments and decide which path I'm going to take.

Life is a journey: physically, mentally, and emotionally. The path you take is an adventure. Explore and experience these challenges for change, realizing they are intertwined. As you do a deep dive within, look at what the future holds and where you want to be. How are you going to process and progress by communication within yourself? Prepare yourself, so you will find viability.

Realize moveable and forceable energy comes from within. Who you take along with you will help determine your path, so weed out the nay-sayers who have held you back. Our past tells us about things behind, our present tells us about things right now, and our future tells us about opportunities and adventures to have. Turning a pissed attitude in to a positive attitude will afford you a sense of balance that will lead you to peace of mind and bring a smile to your face.

Get the pom-poms down and start cheering yourself to the next level. *Why not?*

Cecilia J. Howell-Canada, MD, is a pediatric clinician with an adventurous nature, dedicated to providing quality care to those in need: mentally, physically, and emotionally. She has seen and enjoyed breathtaking scenery as she lived in Alaska, Nevada, Illinois, Wisconsin, and Maryland. Cecilia is a mother, sister, friend, and confidant as well as a motivator, coach, cheerleader, active listener, strategist, reader, baker, and podcaster. She is listed in *Who's Who in America,* 2023 edition. You can contact her at: coach2becoached@gmail.com

CHAPTER 16

You're kidding me, right?

Dr. Diane Kalendra

I was in a mid-career crisis. I'd reached my forties, and I'd achieved a lot by most people's standards. I was an experienced, high-achieving marketing professional with a sense of my own potential. I had worked in large national and international organizations and not-for-profits, as well as entrepreneurial ventures. And, I had recently completed a doctoral degree while working full-time for a government business enterprise.

I was technically skilled at what I did, and I had been developing myself for years. Outwardly, my life looked great, and I had been successful in many ways. However, inside I was feeling uneasy and unfulfilled. That feeling of being on purpose, vitally alive, and fully engaged with life in ways that were deeply meaningful eluded me.

I tried doing more of the same work that had made me outwardly successful, only I tried to do it better: reading more books, listening to more audios, and attending yet more workshops, seminars, and trainings. But, what had worked before was no longer working.

I came across the Japanese concept of *ikigai*. Roughly, it translates to uncovering your *reason for being* or *purpose in life*. You may have heard of it.

It's said in the West to be at the intersection of:

- What you love (your passions, interests and hobbies—the things that make you feel happy and fulfilled)
- What you're good at (your gifts, skills, talents and expertise—the things you excel at and can offer the world)
- What the world needs (the problems or needs that you can solve—the things that can make a positive impact on the world)
- What you can be paid for (what can support your livelihood—the things you can do to earn a living)

More broadly, in Japan, your ikigai can be any motivating force that brings satisfaction, happiness, and meaning to your everyday life (paid or not). Everyone has an ikigai, but your ikigai may be hidden deep inside you.

I desperately wanted to know my ikigai. But, the harder I tried to find it, the more elusive it became. No amount of trying to *figure it out* was helping: not what I was passionate about nor what gifts I could excel at and offer the world and, in turn, would allow me to make a difference in the world, support my livelihood, and have me feel fulfilled. I was not able to find my ikigai.

Exhausted from the mental effort and energetic grasping, I was frustrated. Then, one day, it occurred to me: if I couldn't figure it out, I'd ask in meditation.

What gifts could I offer this world, in exchange for the gifts of this world?

I had practiced meditation for some time. So, I set my intention and settled in. Lying down, palms to my side and turned up, I took a deep breath in—and exhaled. Then, a second breath—in and out. And, finally, a third long, deep breath in with a long, slow, exhale out.

I saw myself walking high up along the ridge of a lush, rolling hill. Looking down through the mist, I could see a lake directly below. Between the lake and me was a gate, and beyond the gate, a gentle path led the way down, amongst tall trees, to the lake.

I opened the gate, walked through it, and closed it behind me. As I continued to walk down the path, I slowly took off the clothes and the metaphorical masks I was wearing in my daily life: personally—as a daughter, a wife, a mother—and professionally. I kicked off my shoes. I unbuttoned my dress, letting it slip off my shoulders and fall, silently, to the ground.

Eventually, I reached the lake and stepped into its stillness, walking out from the shore until I slowly slipped beneath the surface and into its watery depths.

As I floated down, I stopped to look around. Sparkling light from above pierced through the deep blue hues surrounding me. To my surprise and delight, a pod of charming and attentive dolphins was frolicking around me. One stopped and invited me to ride. Graciously, I accepted the invitation. On his back, he carried me at speed, swiftly, down—and yet further down, into the depths of the lake. Eventually, we reached the bottom and a rocky shelf where there was a grotto. A home, with a wooden door.

I approached the door and knocked. Frustrated, and expecting a laundry list of talents, I asked: "What *are* my gifts?"

Suddenly, the door flung open, and a figure appeared. Equally frustrated, it replied: "Why? Don't you know? You *are* the gift!"

As suddenly as it had appeared, the figure disappeared, and the door slammed shut behind it.

Stunned, I stepped back. As this simple truth alchemized, my body relaxed, and I fell backwards. The dolphin swooped behind me, scooped me up, and dutifully carried me back to the shore.

Emerging from the water, I found a beautiful new silk and golden-threaded dress and pair of shoes laid out to wear. I put them on and turned to sit on the sandy shore for a while. Looking back over the lake and into a glorious sunset, I bathed in its golden light and reflected on my strange and wonderous encounter: *If I am the gift, who (or what) is doing the giving?*

In that moment, I remembered who I *really* was (a child of God) and what I was *truly* here to do (extend God's love). *Oh, my gosh! That's it! You're kidding me, right?*

For so long, I had been spinning in my head. Trying to figure it out. Thinking I needed to control everything, or I would be overwhelmed. Thinking I was so small and insignificant, with no real power to make any real difference in the world. Thinking I was failing, and ultimately, fearing I would leave this world feeling unfulfilled.

The truth was that I had all the power of the universe, in me. All I had to do was *show up* (like a gift), so its power could come through me to make *all* the difference in the world. A-maz-ing! And, so very humbling. I found my ikigai.

Now, all I had to do was *figure out* how to live from this new way of thinking. Oops! I caught myself. Trying to figure it out, again. While my newfound truth was simple, it seemed living it was possibly going to be difficult, because it was so radically different.

The next day, an email dropped into my box. It was from Marianne Williamson, and it was about *A Course in Miracles* (Foundation for Inner Peace 1992). I did not really know very much about Marianne, nor did I really know anything much about this course, but my attention was drawn to its introductory invitation.

Marianne warned it was not a course for everyone, but I knew it was for me. In a heartbeat, I became a student of *A Course in Miracles*. One of its principles is living in the present moment. It teaches that the present moment is the only moment that truly exists and that by being fully present in each moment, we can experience greater spiritual awareness.

Paradoxically, the more I stopped trying to take control and relaxed into surrendering control by showing up fully in the present moment and letting go of attachment to the past or future, my life began to transform. While it didn't happen overnight, it did happen.

I transitioned out of my corporate job and into academia. I was told, as a practitioner, I would not be accepted. I showed up anyway. I practiced being in the present moment. I learned how to facilitate teaching teams and classes. I learned how to write learning materials, how to set assignments that assessed learning outcomes, and how to mark seemingly endless numbers of papers. I learned how to do research and supervise research candidates. I learned how to lead academic working groups and supervise academic staff.

It was not always easy, but I drew on my previous professional experience and on remembering who I really was and what I was truly here to do: to simply *be the gift*, fully present for students who were overwhelmed by their study, for staff who were frustrated by the system, and for solving seemingly endless problems.

In my first year, I won a teaching excellence award. Then, I was promoted. And, promoted again. Students and staff were telling me the difference I had made in their lives. I was happy.

I'm frequently asked, "How do you do it?" Now, you know! If you live in the present moment, you will be able to show up and be the gift that makes a difference. Stay focused on the present moment, and you will be able to experience a sense of inner peace and a deeper connection to your true self, and your ikigai.

Wherever you are on your journey right now, whatever you might be going through, I hope (on some level) my sharing this story has helped you remember who you *really* are and what you're *truly* here to do too. (Hint: You *are* the gift too.)

Dr. Diane Kalendra transitioned to academia after twenty-five years' experience as a marketing professional and completing a PhD in organizational change. Since then, Diane has worked with thousands of senior managers, CEOs, board directors, and entrepreneurs to change their lives by developing their competencies and capacities through completing their MBA. Diane's discovered successful organizational (or community) change requires first an understanding of who we are and what we need to become. Connect with Diane at: www.linkedin.com/in/dr-diane-kalendra-2b281911/

CHAPTER 17

Mastering Technique and Artistry of Music in Your Life

Dr. Christine E. Lee

Have you ever wondered if you are doing what you are meant to do? I woke up one morning and asked if there was more to life than what I was doing at the time. I was well-regarded as a physician, made enough income, and had a happy family. Therefore, I should have been satisfied that I was successful.

The question lingered, *Should there be more to life?*

As a mom of three children, I was busy as my kids were growing up. I worked full-time as a physician and surgeon, ran my practice, and raised children. Now that all three kids were successful, thriving, and working out of state, I realized they did not need me as much. My husband also took a job out of state after twenty years of a career here in our hometown. I felt alone for the first time in a long time.

I was expected to move to follow my husband across the country at some point, but I wondered: What would I be doing there? I looked around to find similar jobs in the new city. Of course, there were many jobs in ophthalmology, but the big question kept nagging at me. Would I be fulfilled and happy?

The happiest moments I can remember were when I was on stage playing piano, really connecting to the music, connecting with the audience, in the flow of the moment, feeling alive with passion, and on top of the world. With Beethoven's "Pathétique Sonata," I won and became the finalist in our state Piano Solo and Ensemble competition for two years in a row. However, the highlight was when I was invited to play a musical selection of my favorite piano piece at the Honors Convocation before my high school graduation.

When I was young, I dreamed of becoming a pianist, sharing my gift, and performing. I explored all the emotions the music allowed me to express when playing. The piano transported me to places I could not dare to venture. Unfortunately, I could not pursue my first dream since my parents stopped my piano lessons. My parents told me that I was not meant to be a pianist. I was crushed.

I moved on to college and then to medical school. I decided to be a surgeon. However, piano playing shaped me into an ophthalmologist. Ophthalmic surgeries are delicate and are performed under a microscope. Many times, I used to think that eye surgery was a performance just as precise as classical music, especially the technical parts. Every note needed to be exact, just like eye surgeries.

As an ophthalmologist, I have helped my patients see again after cataracts or refractive surgeries. I enjoyed the surgeries I got to do and considered those surgeries performances, which allowed me to do the best I could. In other words, my stage was the operating room. These events transformed patients' lives, and I have countless stories of grateful patients.

As I pondered my next move, I returned to find myself when I used to be curious, open, and optimistic. Deep down, these traits felt familiar again. I saw more possibilities and opportunities. I also realized that I had coached my kids when they were home through high school. When coaching, I felt a connection with my children in the same way I connected to my piano music. I felt the children's struggles, emotions, and solutions.

As I learned more about coaching, I became more interested and wondered about the possibilities. I welcomed the opportunity. Could I be enthusiastic about it? Could I make transformative differences in my clients' lives? What would that look like? Of course, there are learning curves with any new, potential learning. Would I utilize all my passion, talent, strengths, and identity? I chose coaching as a new profession and decided to receive formal training. Could coaching be the fundamental part of my life that had been missing?

Some of the coaching skills did not come naturally or intuitively to me. For example, my surgeon's mindset—which is analytical, judgmental, and critical—did not work well in the coaching world. I had to unlearn many characteristics of being an accomplished eye surgeon. I had to stop asking all those closed-ended questions and learn how to ask open-ended questions. I had to be more vulnerable to ask thought-provoking, challenging, and solution-focused questions.

I had to slow down. I learned to listen for the tone of voice behind words. I watched facial expressions and body language. I opened my heart to listen to feelings, emotions, and values. Then, I had to quiet my inner brain from its analysis, judgment, and criticism. Whenever I did that, I became more intuitive and felt a connection with my clients. Although some of the processes were challenging, I felt alive when doing them, and watching my clients transform before my eyes was transformative for me. Besides, I did not even need the operating room. *I can do this anywhere*, I thought.

After mastering the technical parts of any music, the next step to complete mastery would be the artistic part. Because ophthalmic surgery is strictly technical, there is no room for creativity or artistry.

Had I been missing this creative part of my life? Was I becoming a glorified technician as an ophthalmologist?

I remembered playing at the Honors Convocation. At the time, I played my favorite composer, Ludwig van Beethoven. His iconic work, known as "Pathétique Sonata in C minor," is loved by many pianists. It starts with a grave tempo, slow and solemn music. It was initially published as "Grande Sonate Pathétique," meaning *big emotional sonata*, as musical historians tell us that *pathos* conveyed emotions in that period. This music is passionate, intense, and even angry at times, with heavy chords that mostly lead to uncertainty. The dynamics of the loudest to softest sounds change suddenly, making the music emotionally unstable as if any emotions are possible. The first movement eventually becomes very fast and contains dialogues in the music, where all possibilities are considered. Quick angry outbursts give way to lovely, soft, and tender sounds, allowing the individual's interpretations to explore other meanings.

The beauty of music is in the interpretation and individualized approach. One of the essential parts of coaching is that people are so different that coaching needs to be personalized to each person's needs and desires. For example, the second movement of the same sonata, "Adagio Cantabile," can feel so different, just as each coaching session may feel different. I found my passion again by using my piano skills to review the coaching process.

My genuine love for piano led me to ophthalmology, but only as far as the technical part of music—accuracy, precision, and exactness. However, when coaching, I feel more alive, engaged, and delighted. This new artistry brought me back to life, full of energy and whole, as if I am once again mastering creativity.

Changing careers can be scary, but figuring out what you are passionate about can help you. For me, I had to figure out what used to excite me. If I can allow my clients to make those transformative differences through coaching, that can be my mission.

Now, I am passionate about coaching. I am creating new performances with coaching, with my life's technical and artistic components. Creating performances in my mind is art, like music. The key to excellent coaching is personalizing the work to individuals, needs, and desires. This aligns with my philosophy of coaching, the power of choices, and being intentional about your choices so that you are focused and have clarity.

If you are not doing what you are meant to do, then deep down, you may feel that something is missing and sense emptiness in your life. Returning to my happiest moments, I found the joy of artistry. Music without artistry is music without a soul.

Of course, you cannot return to the past, and much time has passed. I had denied a part of me, like my emotional part. Are you ignoring a part of yourself or not utilizing all of your potential? Whatever it may be, once I accepted all of myself, I became engaged, fulfilled, and more satisfied. We all have unique strengths, experiences, and visions that create significance and meaning in our lives.

Figuring out your current options is the key to expressing yourself and finding happiness. Do not be afraid to explore; it is never too late to find yours, even if it takes work, since you will find your purpose and passion. I wish you the joy of life when you find what you are meant to do.

Life is a series of performances—All put together!

Christine E. Lee, MD, is a physician, speaker, and certified executive professional coach. Dr. Lee coaches professionals, especially educational and medical professionals, to become the best version of themselves and to positively impact others. She guides clients to align with their intention, purpose, and values. She graduated from the University of Michigan's Honors Program in Philosophy and

Molecular Biology, the University of Michigan Medical School, and the University of Virginia's ophthalmology residency. Contact Dr. Lee at her website: christineleemd.com.

CHAPTER 18

Still, I Live

Deborah Liverett

Mothering and cooking are my expressions of love and the ways I inspire people. I feed them and myself with my secret sauce, cooking with love in my heart, which often delights our senses and opens us up to deeper conversations. When either of these expressions are interrupted, new perceptions must be born—based on the faith foundation in which I stand.

When the unthinkable becomes an unbearable reality, where do you turn? How do you decide what to do?

The answers are varied and buried deeply within each of us. I share my deeply personal survival journey in hopes that it may inspire you should you ever have to make the decision: *Shall I choose to live?*

At lunch, a dear friend—who is more of a sister—asked if would I write about the ways I came to cope and deal with the tragedy of my youngest son's sudden death in 2020. I had three ready reasons why that would not happen. I can't recall any of them now because they were my bogus protection tactics to shut down the conversation.

She shook her head in understanding and kindly let the conversation drop after she said, "You have done such a fine job of handling the impossible."

Fast forward to the next morning when I saw an email asking if I had a transformational story to share in an anthology. The awareness was immediate; the Universe was behind her comment as a primer, if you will, which would allow me to share my deeply personal survival journey to lift and inspire others. Writing this chapter is what I was called to do, so the only answer that made sense was to say yes.

The first holiday after the death of my son, I chose to interact with a small group of people and refused to answer any questions I did not want to answer. My goal was to simply be in the moment. The second and third holidays, I had some okay moments and very sad moments, shedding many hidden holiday tears in the bathroom or trying to recover in the bedroom. I survived by reminding myself to be grateful for the forty years and three weeks that I shared with my son.

I spent a few months of staying by myself, going to bed when I needed to because sleep often alluded me, and standing only when necessary. Then, I turned back to yoga and meditation. I collected therapists' names and their phone numbers. I even added a hypnotist to the list. I reminded myself to not push feelings down or to ignore them. I sat in those feelings and told myself: *It takes as long as it takes because feelings of grief are pained and layered.*

As well-meaning people asked, "How are you?" I honored where I was with a response born of that very moment. I told the truth, no matter what it was. "I'm okay," I might say, but I reserved the right to not be okay in the next moment.

I sometimes needed to cover my head under my weighted blanket when the hard-to-breathe days appeared. That seemed the kindest way to honor my feelings, and the kinder I was to myself, the kinder I could be to others. I learned never to shy away the from heartbreak moments, and I didn't linger in them longer than I needed to.

There were people who didn't know what to say, when to stop asking questions, or who said too much. They just didn't know any better. I had to detach from their words, stating clearly and at times forcefully that I couldn't talk any longer. I often needed to hang up to allow myself time to find compassion for their well-meaning. These moments required me to venture back to my spiritual grounding, knowing that God is my source and my foundation in sorrow as well as in joy. That slight glimmer of remembering became my turning point, but my recovery took longer.

What once relaxed me wasn't working. I had no appetite for cooking or photography or visiting with people. I was no longer who I was nor how I once saw myself. At this point, I realized it was time to choose: *Shall I wither away and merely exist, or shall I decide to truly live?*

When the weight of living inside sorrow's marrow piles on top of me, I seek out what I need to do to forgive myself and others. Judgment of myself and others was becoming a weapon of destructive force. Judgment and healing cannot exist in the same recipe. Judgment is our distorted viewpoint of truth.

When people are involved, the truth is nebulous, seen by each person from their myopic vantage point. I feel blessed to be able to see multiple sides of situations. When I see other people's pain and how they cope, they are often different from my own coping mechanisms. So, the goal became for me to see the love in each person rather than their attachment to fear, which distorts and destroys any recipe for living. Fear seeks to protect itself by whispering about the wrongs of others, cutting us off from seeing the humanity within each of us.

I was cutting myself off from one person in particular. It took me a few years to see that I forgave everyone except one person. I continued to hold the grudge that kept a wedge between us. I justified it in my mind by telling myself we had never been truly close anyway. Then one Christmas, I saw a picture of the person, and I knew it was time to lift the veil that was distorting my ability to see clearly. By holding the grudge, I was holding onto a sliver of pain that was preventing complete acceptance. That shift blew like a tea kettle whistle, allowing that long-held perception to dissolve in my mind and heart. I extended the last bit of compassion, not only to that person but ultimately to myself.

Every lesson, every relationship is a reason to remember to Love. Energetically, I exchanged hurt for love through an alchemy of acceptance that freed me to return completely to my original state, Love—and Love is available to all of us.

I allow myself to feel what I feel to this day. Whenever the more haunting feelings show up, I allow myself to feel them. As time moves forward, the hauntings do not last as long. The feeling arises, and I let the tear fall. It's like a cat who walks into the room, is satisfied you are still there, then walks out of the room.

The role of acceptance still plays an important role in my own radical transformation. I think: *Where can I apply compassion in my inner voice's chatter?* I remember that compassion for others leads to space to have compassion for myself—even as my darkest thoughts about *What could I have done better?* begin to boil over. Everyone was or is struggling with something. My trust lies in the state of *agape*, the spiritual love between humans. Either we are agape in action, or we are in the need of receiving agape.

If you create space to surrender to the new order of things, you will discover a peaceful transfer into a new way of thinking, feeling, and behaving.

As a lover of cooking, I know the importance of order when you add ingredients or when choosing to stir versus whip your mixture. Life, I have found, does not have a neat order. There is no handy recipe for living it when insurmountable pain constricts our ability to think, remember details, or filter our reactions.

There were, however, key ingredients to my recovery that I share in hopes they will aid you in your journey.

I have coined them FACTS:

F = Feel/Faith/Forgiveness

A = Acceptance

C = Change/Choose/Compassion

T = Trust/Truth Telling

S = Surrender

Feeling what you feel takes **faith**, an assurance that you will survive. **Forgiveness** frees us to be our less encumbered self.

Acceptance delivers us from the fight of what *was* into the now of what *is*.

Change your perception to thoughts that do not crush your spirit so that you may live on. **Choose** wisely not wildly, which requires you to lay down any judgement of yourself and others. **Compassion** for others leads to compassion for yourself.

Our ability to **trust** in something greater than ourselves allows us to sit in and share our **truth telling** of who we are, how we are, and how we wish to evolve.

Surrender is letting go of wishful thinking for what *was* so that we may embrace the nuance of what *is*.

These FACTS have helped me be myself, be good to myself, choose new directions, and say yes to new challenges, such as climbing Lion's Head Mountain in Cape Town, South Africa, last Christmas.

My wish for you, dear reader, is that you gain an awareness of your ability to recover and that you now know you can choose your direction. May you decide: *Still, I live*.

Deborah Liverett is a faith-filled mother, grandmother, and maternal figure to many. She is a Certified Life Coach who inspires people to practice self-care while shining their unique power to enhance our world. She is a lover of cooking, reading, traveling, and photography. She retired from a successful corporate career helping underserved global communities and graduated Magna Cum Laude from North Carolina Central University. She can be reached at @deborahliverett on Instagram.

CHAPTER 19

It's Never Enough

Joe Mirachi

Have you ever felt that despite an impressive list of accomplishments, it was never enough, and you still had something to prove? Or, when you reach a goal, do you barely take time to celebrate before shifting your focus to the next destination to conquer? I had already exceeded everyone's expectations—including mine—yet it was never enough. The perpetual big chase to the next accomplishment began with me, and I suddenly understood why and was ready for a change.

I was raised in a modest-income household with alcoholism and other dysfunctional behaviors. I lacked connection and a sense of belonging in my upbringing, which made me feel alienated as I moved into my teenage years. I resolved to overcome these shortcomings, and the difficulties of my youth fueled a determination that continued to drive and motivate me for decades.

I worked my way through college and began my career. Although occasionally plagued with self-doubts, I offset this mindset by working hard and seeking opportunities to advance my career and value. With every promotion, I felt compelled to up my game and worked even harder to prove myself. I thought I would stay ahead of the game as long as I could out-work everyone else. I sold my natural abilities short and saw my success as primarily a result of hard work.

Being open to continuous learning and relocation opportunities, I advanced to a CEO position by the age of fifty. Despite being a successful CEO, I continued to covet the next potential accomplishment, including speaking engagements and board positions. *Perhaps I'll even write a book*, I thought. There was always another hill to conquer or dragon to slay as I continued pushing myself to higher performance levels.

I constantly compared myself to other people, especially anyone that appeared to have something I lacked. Shrugging off my accomplishments, my life was never enough. Then in my early sixties, my turning point moment arrived.

Years ago, I heard of imposture syndrome and recognized I had some tendencies, such as a lack of confidence, a reluctance to take risks, and a fear of failure. However, over time I pushed back against the feelings of self-doubt and lack of confidence by doubling down on hard work and perseverance. Such doubts became almost a blessing, motivating me to greater heights. As my accomplishments grew, my self-doubts faded into the background, although they never completely disappeared.

I was compelled to re-examine imposture syndrome when I read an article linking it to high achievers who experienced a lack of belonging in their formative years. Bingo! That was me. I had somehow thought my achievements were evidence I had overcome imposture syndrome when, in fact, it was evidence of its downside and hidden costs. Imposture syndrome fueled an initially helpful cycle that, over time, had become counterproductive. What was new was the recognition that high achievers could suffer from imposture syndrome. I began to see where this condition served me and where it had not. I saw where my mental processes entrapped me into a cycle of accomplishments—a nagging feeling of still needing to prove myself, an ongoing sense that *it's never enough*.

For me, the name *imposture syndrome* is a bit deceptive. I did not feel that I was fake or untrue to myself; instead, persistent feelings of being an outsider generated a general sense of anxiety—like the feeling one gets playing musical chairs and being the one left standing when the music stops. At times this feeling made me reluctant to share with others—not because I was an imposture—but because I was uncomfortable with the potential reaction of rejection I might receive. This discomfort was especially acute when I proposed an unconventional understanding of an issue because I might be ostracized as an outsider, reopening the wound of lacking a sense of belonging in this world.

Suddenly, I looked at imposture syndrome as a liability rather than as a source of motivation. Despite having accomplished more than my expectations, I realized I remained focused on what I had not yet achieved. My point of view dramatically shifted as I recognized that imposture syndrome had more significant consequences than a few quirks in my personality. I also realized this issue resulted from my mental processes, and it was up to me to resolve it. Ironically, despite transforming many aspects of my life and overcoming many facets of my upbringing, I realized I was still struggling with family-of-origin issues. What's old is new again.

This revelation generated questions to reflect on, such as:

- How do I overcome these remaining legacies of my upbringing?
- How do I leverage this newfound understanding into action?
- Where do I redirect my passion for learning and personal growth?
- How do I change my way of thinking to overcome imposture syndrome?

This new perspective led to different choices. Instead of coveting them, I declined opportunities to serve on boards and advisory committees. I realized my resume was already impressive and did not lack a thing. It represented an admirable career after my unimpressive beginnings. I was ready to release the needs to conquer the next challenge and to continue to seek accolades and accomplishments.

I found it helpful to reframe limiting thoughts as they arose to prevent them from becoming embedded in a fixed mindset. Combined with a practice of gratitude, the *it's never enough* mentality began to lose its hold.

Moreover, I had a job I enjoyed, excelled in, and found full of meaning and purpose. Initially, in my career, I developed myself to advance my career, and this gradually shifted to developing others' over time. I now see a large part of my job as facilitating human potential and cultivating an organization of learning and development that gives my work meaning and purpose.

Upon reflection, I ascertained that the best way to transform my thinking was to work on my spiritual development. Although I felt the pull to develop my spiritual side as an adolescent, this was overtaken by my practical nature and the desire to become a financially independent adult. As a result, this latest *Turning Point* evolved from an insight into a spiritual quest. Having transformed much of the externally valued aspects of my life, I now set forth on an inward transformation. Always more spiritual than religious, the timing was perfect.

Although continuing to work full time, my personal development took a distinct turn. Instead of participating in career-focused development opportunities, I returned to school to pursue spiritual studies. Recalling my youthful wandering in the woods, I again set out to explore and develop my spiritual nature. I am excited and invigorated to reconnect with my spiritual aspirations and look forward to new understandings and turning points in my journey to overcome the remnants of imposture syndrome.

Your life is filled with turning points and transformations, and you actively participate in the process. You co-create your life by asking questions, learning, and changing your perspective. Transformation is a complicated and continuous process with direction and momentum, but it typically does not follow a linear path. To quote the adage: *When the student is ready, the teacher arrives.*

Build on your strengths in making transitions and proceed with the end in mind. A transformation is a fundamental change that begins with letting go of existing beliefs, understandings, and paradigms. You can also include letting go of an identity and connection to a group or cause. The change begins with you.

The need to be open-minded is central to turning points and transformations. A key indicator of open-mindedness is accepting that an intelligent and good-hearted individual can hold a different opinion than you regarding a topic. If you are not open-minded on an issue, then change in that area is impossible.

Your life is a series of turning points and transitions. As you move to the next chapter, you must be willing to let go of your current understanding. Just as winter foreshadows the new growth of spring, your personal development is preceded by the release or death of prior knowledge or identity. Doubt is the soil from which a new understanding, and new life, can grow.

Let go and let grow!

Joe Mirachi is the CEO of Launch Credit Union, and his professional profile is available on LinkedIn. A lifelong learner, his academic background includes an economics degree, an MBA, and several years facilitating college classes in economics, marketing, finance, and strategic planning. A systems thinker, Joe excels at synthesizing ideas into practical frameworks. He is married and resides in Florida.

CHAPTER 20

Love Saves The Day

Erika Morrell

"Tut, tut, child!" said the Duchess. "Everything's got a moral, if you can only find it."
—Lewis Carroll, *Alice's Adventure in Wonderland*

Our story, as you will see, is no exception.

Life is very interesting sometimes; you get to where you are meant to be in ways you never would have expected, under circumstances you never could have imagined. These situations always contain that critical moment—a *turning point*—where the choices you make and how you show up define your life.

The sixth of March, 2007, started out like any other day. We had recently moved to Los Angeles from New York City, a move I would have never imagined making as I was born and raised in the city. I considered myself a diehard New Yorker and was proud of it. That night, I was conducting my first LA workshop, *Living Metaphysics,* a workshop I had led a hundred times or more. Fueled by the sold-out crowd and the desire to prove to myself and the audience that my change in coast would not change my work, I was resolved to make this my best workshop to date, living up to the audience's expectations.

Leaving a little shop on Ventura Boulevard armed with the *have to have* statue of Cupid and Psyche, I felt assured the set would be perfect. I started making my way toward my rented silver Ford Explorer. Suddenly, I could not take a step; my feet were as heavy as cement. I leaned against the building, trying to assess my situation. Was I having a panic attack? A heart attack? A stroke? Was I dying? I was terrified.

Born what I term *multi-dimensionally sensitive*, I have always spent my life living by Source, inspiration, and intuition. I have had a relationship with God, Angels, and all Divine beings throughout my life—what I lovingly referred to as *They*—and *They* had never let me down. We had been through a lot throughout my life: a blood incompatibility with my Mother (a 50/50 chance whether I would be born) in utero, a breech birth, the doctor cutting my left heel off by accident while administering my first inoculation, asthma attacks, car crashes, bouts of walking pneumonia, allergies, fire, and 9/11, just to name a few.

There had been more than numerous times throughout my life I was directed, protected, and saved by my Cosmic Team. I was once asked how I felt being so unlucky; I had to correct them. I considered and still consider myself one of the luckiest, most blessed people in the world to have had so many learning experiences. I am sure if I heard your story, I would consider you the same. We are lucky.

Miraculously, under the eyes of God and the Angles, I made my way home. I was scared, confused, and frightened, yet at the same time oddly peaceful. I started to meditate and pray, looking for direction and understanding. My answers came from above: Was I dying? *No.* Did I need to go to the hospital? *No.* I exhaled a sigh of relief. What was happening to me? *A lesson*. I could do a lesson.

I had a successful career in private practice as a metaphysician and healer since graduating from college in 1990. My clientele had been high-end, and I had appeared in almost all the notable newspapers and magazines. When I moved to California, I had bigger dreams. I wanted to make a bigger impact and serve in a bigger way, sharing all of my wisdom, knowledge, and gifts. Now what was I going to do? Who was I going to choose to be?

I had a choice: who was I going to be as a product of that change in mobility? At that point in the history of the world, showing up in person still mattered. I made the choice that I was still going to show up as me—powerful, present, and purposeful. Most people did not even know about the walking challenge.

I did not hide it; I just did not make it an issue. I sat a lot, using a desk chair to transport myself from one place to the next. I was escorted a lot, allowing my weight and balance to be shared with others. And I always showed up as me.

Intention is powerful, and so is surrender. Before I had too much time to think about it, Divine Intervention held my hand and led the way. I did not cancel my workshop; I just sat the entire time. Shortly after that, I received an offer to appear on Bravo's *Millionaire Matchmaker*. Then I was offered a number of speaking gigs, other TV appearances, and a show on LA Talk Radio. My audience was growing—so were my client numbers and so was my income.

The multitude of gifts that arose from my change in mobility were many and impacted all areas of my life in positive ways. I had to learn to stop holding the energy of *doing*. As a New Yorker, life was all about the *doing*: how many places could you show up, how many people could you meet, how many hands could you shake, how fabulously could you show up, and most importantly, how fast. Now the energy became about *allowing*, moving slower (no pun intended), being more mindful of every moment. I was observing what was being shown to me and how I was being asked to show up—in what ways and for whom.

I developed a new relationship with my body. I never really had much of a relationship with my body, except like most women around weight. My esoteric life held the majority of my focus, especially as I was defined as sickly. Always dealing with, managing, or fighting something off, my spirituality and all my esoteric gifts held my power, so that was where I focused most of the time. In my new reality, what I ate, how I moved, what I wore, and what I cleaned with mattered a great deal. My body was constantly talking to me by feeling better, worse, weaker, or stronger.

I become aware of my thoughts and words to a greater level, even though I would have never thought that was possible. I already understood that every thought becomes a thing and that words amplify our ideas, but I became super conscious of my thoughts and words, putting out into the ether *only* what I wanted, only the direction I wanted to take.

One of the biggest gifts I received was learning how to allow people to help me, an idea I had never considered. I had to learn to be vulnerable and allow that word to also contain being strong, so as not to hold the energy of a victim.

Yes, I had friends, boyfriends, and employees, but I had always played the role of the healer and psychic. In the role of someone looking for a little support, I had to redefine what being in charge of my life looked like and the roles others played in it. Self-sufficient now meant something different; it was now more what I held as a collaboration. By allowing the love that I moved through the world with, I was allowing myself to receive from others.

Without question, the greatest gift that came out of the change in mobility was the gift of self-love. We all believe we love ourselves, and I would say that was true to a certain degree. The circumstances thrust on me brought moments that were very dark—moments I needed to look to the light and focus on love, moments that taught me to rise up and choose myself and the life I wanted and was meant to live. I never lost focus of that, not once, no matter what I was feeling.

My faith saved my life on more than one occasion. I forgave myself for things I had not known bothered me, and others for ways they hurt me. I expressed my love to others and life in a greater way, beyond what I thought was possible. I defined myself in each moment I was living, choosing how I was going to show up. I observed myself and life, constantly fine-tuning both, aligning myself and my behaviors with my beliefs, values, understandings, and deepest desires.

I lost my ability to walk unaided for a little over seventeen years. I did not, in any way, lose my ability to live. This temporary loss of something that defined me in so many ways allowed me to show up for myself and the world in ways I could never have imagined.

How are you living your majesty? What choices are you making?

Pay no attention to how it *should be* based on your storyline; choose what you will have it be despite your storyline. Whatever you're facing—no matter what—choose yourself and Love.

Be all you can be, and more. I believe in you!

Erika Morrell is a doctor of Philosophy of Metaphysical Sciences. Her Los Angeles-based company, Knowledgeable Soul, LLC, is committed to evolving a spiritually-centered existence. Through her writing, teaching, and speaking, she educates, aligns, and enlightens others, creating a conscious awareness of Universal dynamics and their practical applications. You can hear her weekly on LA Talk Radio or on her daily podcast, *Loves Saves the Day with Erika Morrell*. Get to know Erika at: www.LoveErika.com

CHAPTER 21

Tongue-Tied Minute

Blanche Moskovici

TIA Awakening

On April 19, 2022, while seated with a family caregiver and feeling grateful, I experienced a possible *transient ischemic attack* (TIA) or mini stroke. I felt caught off guard, surprised. Instinctively, I connected with my breath in the silence. While this felt so real, it made no sense to me, given my family health history. Since then, Divine Grace has been guiding my path, inspiring me to shift my career and life direction. I am now called to share this experience with you as it consolidated many years of intuitive and creative wisdom, personal development and therapy, meditation, mindfulness, mindset training, and Qigong energy arts practice into one minute of time, literally.

What Happened

While talking with my client virtually, my tongue suddenly tightened towards my right inner cheek. If you have ever heard the expression being *tongue-tied*, this is exactly what it felt like.

My thoughts could not form into sentences. Words came out as mumbled sounds, and what I heard myself enunciate did not match my thoughts. The sound of slurred words reverberated my being, and I was incited to slow down and breathe. I looked at her and chose to turn my gaze inward, like I have done many times before while practicing *zazen*. Yet for me, this moment of silence in gratitude took on a different flavor.

In one rapid moment, my focus shifted *to being aware of myself in space, as well as my body*. I knew the importance of staying calm in a stressful situation. I chose next to *lay my fear aside*, mustering all my inner strength and years of self-awareness practice to *check in with myself* to see if I could turn my tongue clockwise.

Despite failing on the first attempt, I took another deep breath and brought my focus to the new present moment. This is the power of mind, in that energy flows where your attention goes. Gazing at my client briefly, I saw no reaction. My facial features had not changed. Did I need to say anything? No. Self-care was of utmost importance. I returned my focus inward in gratitude.

Glimpses of Possibility

I thought about prior successful experiences in applying this technique with other pain points in the body in which they would release almost instantaneously. In each new present moment, I recognized the opportunity to embrace a new lived experience. First, *I shed the light of consciousness on my tongue, as well as the space around it*. Next, *I guided myself with a loving compassionate question*, by asking: "Can I turn my tongue clockwise? Yes, I can." Fully present, *I listened to how my tongue responded to my instruction* to turn clockwise. I felt as if I were passing a spiritual exam, learning how to *trust, let go, and flow* on the fly. A sigh of relief. Yes. What I was doing was working. The circular motion flowed more easily. *This is a new present moment*. I could now get my tongue back online. Wow, what a minute!

I needed to engage with my client, so *I instructed my tongue to speak.* The words came out with effort, somewhat mumbled. I regrouped and took several deep breaths. *Maintaining a state of relaxation was key.* The thought arose, "No matter how I sound, I am able to speak." *I trusted that I could do it,* so I came out of the silence and engaged in a dialogue with her for another five minutes. With each spoken phrase, my articulation improved. In a state of *deep gratitude, feeling thankful* for being able to complete the session in good spirits, we said our goodbyes.

Fear into Flow, Tears of Joy

Once our session concluded, I shared what just happened with my spouse André—and that it freaked me out. Of course, by this point I could speak and articulate well. Still, I decided to call 911, wanting to make sure that all systems were in order.

During my three-day hospital stay, I kept my spirits up and even practiced some Qigong, an ancient Chinese healing art that can transform vital energy flow in the subtle energy body, also known as the etheric body or field. I underwent many tests, only to be told that I may have had a mini stroke or possibly a blood clot that passed and became dislodged in my brain. The doctors were not sure of the cause of my symptoms. I was prescribed meds for cholesterol and to prevent stroke, which I chose not to take for a variety of reasons. Considering the lack of aftereffects, I decided instead to pursue a natural route to improve my health, recognizing alternative medicine as more aligned with who I am.

Trusting myself, I decided to continue with my Qigong energy arts practice to heal. I am certified in Satori Qigong: The Flow Form. As a sidenote, Qi means *energy* and Gong means *work* or *play*, so Qigong is about working with the energy flowing in the Universe, in nature, and in the body—for example, sending love energy to clear energy blockages in the subtle energy field around my tongue.

I also took three months off from psychotherapy private practice to recover, while continuing to work four days per week as a family mental health counselor. The gift of time off, after having worked six-day weeks for the previous three years, was a godsend. In taking this much needed break, something wonderful happened. I experienced Qi energy in a new way. It was during this recovery period that I found my calling.

Ten months later, as I am birthing this introductory chapter to my book, I continue to reflect on and consolidate what happened. Expression plays an integral part in the work I do as an intuitively guided therapist, family mental health counselor, and coach. Without my tongue to communicate, who would I be? At age sixty-one, I realize I haven't yet achieved what I've dreamed of creating. Something else had to shift in my life.

I started to share my *Fab3 Process* with a handful of women in my circle who are familiar with some form of energy arts practice, including Qigong, Tai Chi, and Reiki. This process fuses therapist skills, zen focus, and energy arts practice with awareness to release all sorts of pain, from physical discomfort to emotionally-charged memories and more. With time off came space to just be myself, enjoy life, and heal. New possibilities opened for creative intuitive exploration and play. My process evolved, as did I.

Even today, I feel blessed. I now practice my *Fab3 Process* daily to connect with my Soul. For the first time in my life, I feel like I have something unique to offer, a signature three-step process that works. Tears of joy!

Soul Vision to Inspired Action

When I started this journey to become a therapist, I dreamed of integrating my intuition with a Creative Arts Therapies, MA. I had left behind my intuitive consulting business to begin a new life with a man I love, André. I also left on the shelf a baby project called *Invoking Passion*, that included an audio cassette I asked Dr. Wayne Dyer to review. He wrote me back on January 30, 1993, saying:

> Blanche,
> I encourage you to send the tape + get on with making it PUBLIC.
>
> All Love + Light,
> Wayne

It took me thirty years of being immersed in therapy work and one minute of being tongue-tied to finally listen and reconnect with my Soul vision. I am now inspired to show up, share my message, and be of service as I am.

On January 21, 2023, just before Valentine's Day, I offered my very first *Invoking Passion* online event, surrounded by six good friends, all trained therapists, who care about me succeeding. All I needed to do was take one baby step and initiate my offering to friendly faces. Next, I was guided to complete this chapter. And now, I am on purpose launching my online business, Therapeutic Flow, with Soul guidance, goosebumps, and the *Fab3 Process* lighting my heart path.

What lights you up?

Have you ever played hide and seek with yourself? Imagine for a moment that connecting with your Soul is a gentle and easy process. How would it feel to lay your fear aside, stay open to each new moment, and move beyond feeling tongue-tied in any area of your life? What first step would you take? If not now, what is holding you back? Like me, you may have experienced a frightening life event or several. Remember, healing is a process.

Revisit my pearls of wisdom in *italics* in the above paragraphs.

I invite you to take a leap of faith, trust yourself, move forward, and touch the heart of what lights you up. Offer yourself the gift of *All Love + Light* in this new moment of possibility. It is your turn to shine.

Many blessings,
Blanche

Blanche Moskovici, MA, is a Creative Arts Therapist and Alignment Coach who helps sensitive women embrace new possibilities to self-heal from the pain and overwhelming impact of family mental illness, so they can create a brighter future that lights them up and inspires others. She received her MA in Creative Arts Therapies from Concordia University, Montreal, in 2006 and is a licensed psychotherapist. Her signature *Fab3 Process* is a separate service, not billed under psychotherapy. Email Blanche at: blanche@therapeuticflow.ca or you can visit her at www.therapeuticflow.ca

CHAPTER 22

Opening the Gifts of Care

Paramjit Oberoi

Have there been times in your life when you feel a magical, unexplainable force is the wind beneath your wings? I invite you accompany me through my most intimate moments and to accept my intention of supporting you at your lowest ebb.

Dr. J, the private doctor, gave us the news. I held my husband's hands and burst into tears. He continued, "I'm sorry, Mrs. Oberoi, but this is the beginning of your tears. It's terminal."

I remember my response, "Dr. J, are you not also going to die?"

"Mrs. Oberoi, you are in shock. It will take some time to come to terms with this devastating news."

I remember holding my husband's right hand as we walked out of Dr. J's mansion along the pebbled pathway and supporting my husband into the front seat of our car. Driving home, my husband asked me why I was crying. In that moment, I was glad his technical English was not 100 percent.

My recollection of sitting in Sainsbury's carpark having chosen six books from our local library that had even a slight mention of the disease—remains with me to this day. Those five hours were spent without food and water to sustain me in the car park; I was sick in my stomach with what I was reading.

In simple language, Huntington's disease (HD) is a hereditary disease. Every child of the parent who carries the gene has a 50–50 chance of inheriting the disease. The life expectancy is between fifteen to twenty years from diagnosis. At the time of his diagnosis, we were ten years into our marriage and had three beautiful children.

My mind was doing somersaults; one moment I was going blank, and in the next, my head was spinning, creating future scenarios of doom and gloom.

Holding this diagnosis of Huntington's disease secretly inside me, trying to act as normal as possible with my husband and my children, took me away from being my authentic self. I built a brick wall around myself and operated on autopilot. My insides felt dead, and yet I had a responsible career and family to look after. I truly understood the meaning of *sink or swim*.

I kept the diagnosis hidden from everyone. In fact, I went through so many phases, including *if I don't think about, it will go away*. I was in denial. I felt a deep sense of loss, isolation, and shame. It felt like my whole world had collapsed. I had developed a split personality, trying not to allow my home life affect my work life.

Back in 1987, I was expecting our third child. Our business had gone downhill. To keep a roof over our head, we purchased a chewing gum machine business. We discovered this was a scam and were £15,000 worse off. With a baby on the way, our shop not thriving, and hubby growing more tired, we had no option but to sell the shop. Two weeks before giving birth, we sold our shop and had nowhere to live.

I spoke to my boss, Assistant Director of Social Services, and told him we had put a deposit down for a house, but it would be three months before we could move in. He kindly arranged for us to stay in a staff flat of an old people's home until we moved to our home in July 1988. My faith was restored in human nature.

From that moment, things began to shift. I realized support is available and that I had to be available to receive it. Through desperation, I asked for support and realized I had been living from a place of ego. I hadn't realized the strength in being vulnerable. This tough phase shifted my mindset. I had been brought up with: *Don't share your dirty linen in public. Put on a brave front and deal with the obstacles you face.*

I had a new baby. I thought I was the glue holding the family together. After realizing I was *nobody,* my faith in the divine Universal power grew stronger. I never realized this until that moment that everything instilled from my family was now bearing fruit in terms of my faith in action.

This turning point for me was a month after my son was born. Something pushed me to get up and pick up pen and paper, which I fortunately had by my bedside. Within twenty minutes, I'd written twenty poems. It was like a stream of consciousness. If I close my eyes now, I can visualize the words falling onto the page and my hand hurting from holding the pen so tight. I felt if I didn't hold the pen tightly, I would lose my words. However, on reflection it was never about holding on—it was all about letting go.

When the pressure cooker burst and the tsunami of words hit the page, I realized it was the Universe's way of supporting me, helping me offload onto the page and regain my sanity. I had never written a poem in my life. I had no idea of the depth of pain and anguish I was carrying. I thank the Universal energy for enabling me to purge, let go, and release what was inside me. I had blocked and frozen my emotions as that was the only way I could operate on a minute-by-minute basis.

The first poem was titled "my Piara pen Piara," meaning *love.*

Journaling daily was my saving grace. I developed a love affair with my pen as it understood my feeling and thoughts. The more the paper filled with ink, the lighter I felt. My pen listened, made no judgements, supported me to reflect and face reality with the cushion of knowing that my pen and paper would be there to support me when I fell.

I shifted from feeling sorry for myself and blaming others. This new-found energy and attitude—shifting from victim to victory—gave me the impetus to get up every morning and look my husband and children in the eye, knowing I would do everything in my power to make a difference to raise awareness of this disease and work toward finding a cure.

My husband passed in October of 2002. Many years later, a friend of mine gave me a book called *Why Me, Why This, Why now?* by Robin Norwood (Arrow Books 2009). This influenced my thinking as I reframed my life: Who did I think I was to be exempt from problems in my life? Something inside me changed.

My habit of journaling continues to this day. I am alone but never feel lonely. Because I felt heard by the grace of the Universal essence when journaling, my strength and courage grew.

My middle child was diagnosed with juvenile Huntington's disease (JHD) a day after her daddy's funeral. Twenty years later, my daughter Sheenam can no longer talk or walk and is fed through a tube. She is dependent on twenty-four-hour care to meet her needs.

This journey has taught me enough to fill a whole book; however, if I distill what I have gained from this journey, here are some of the nuggets:

1. Once you get out of your own way, the Universe conspires to support you.
2. When you place God, light, or Universal power in the pilot seat and become the passenger, the journey is made more enjoyable and less bumpy. *Let go and let God.*
3. The tenacity and depth of the human spirit knows no bounds. Whenever you think you have nothing to give, there is still a reservoir from which you can give.

4. When I gave in, I realized I hadn't given up.
5. Cherish every moment. These moments become our memories.
6. Use your experience to support others. We set up a charity called Sheenam's Wish (sheenamswish.co.uk) to support other young people with juvenile Huntington's disease.
7. Facing the reality of death enabled me to embrace it, be less fearful, and to value life. We are all going to die. We just don't know where, when, or how. None of us get out of here alive.

If you are going through difficult times in your life, I urge you to be humble enough to ask for support and not suffer in silence. Opening to trusted family or friends can alleviate your own burdens and enable others to partake in what humans want to do: care and support.

Know that with every challenge there is a gift wrapped up in sandpaper if we can develop the eyes and grace to see it.

Having accumulated over fifty years of caring in my bank, the greatest gift I've been given is to be the beneficiary of the gift of caring. The opportunities and growth through these years have taught me so much and have molded me to be the person I am today. I am the most blessed person on this earth.

Paramjit Oberoi is a woman who walks in faith, courage, and acceptance in equal measures. She wishes to encourage others to find this in their own situations. She is a widow, mother, and end-of-life facilitator who has found her strength and skills from witnessing and supporting three generations of family members with HD and JHD. Her desire is to bring comfort and hope to others on this shared journey. Contact Paramjit at: paramjito@hotmail.com, sheenamswish.co.uk, or LinkedIn @paramjitoberoi

CHAPTER 23

Living a Breakthrough Transformation

Raymond Perras

My Internal Conflict

It was October 1986. I was sitting on a ledge on my way up the Matterhorn in Switzerland. The sky was bright, the view breathtaking. I felt myself held in the hands of a supreme being, part of this wonderful immensity. Not a cloud was in the sky as I beheld the unbelievable mountain sights I had dreamed about for so many years. Climbing part way up the Matterhorn was a dream come true.

Yet, inside me was torment, pain, disillusion, broken trust, and disbelief as I wondered what to do next. Sitting there, I was pondering whether to end it all or face the fact that my marriage was broken. It would be easy to stop the pain for good and just let myself fall down a crack in the mountainous terrain, never to be found. No one knew I had decided that morning to climb up the foothills of the Matterhorn. My troubles would be over forever.

Working Through the Pain

The trip to the Matterhorn was a turning point in my life. I was living through a difficult marriage break up. Thinking that marriage was for life, I was faced with the reality that my wife wanted out. I was seriously asking: *Where to from here?*

We had three beautiful children, ages fourteen, thirteen, and eight. Life was good. I was climbing the corporate ladder. She was entering back into her nursing profession after being a stay-at-home mom.

Living in the suburbs, we enjoyed life as a young family. School, community sports, friends, vacations and summer camps, music and dance lessons—we had everything we needed to be happy. As a couple, we enjoyed romantic dinners and other uplifting outings at special shared moments. I was in great physical shape, running almost every day and even competing in long distance runs. I also did my share of coaching for my kids in soccer, football, and baseball.

Life was beautiful. It was all one could wish for, or so it seemed. I had it made in life.

Unfortunately, the foundation was crumbling. We had a trial separation three years before. By mutual agreement, we got back together. I thought we had dodged a bullet and were ready to continue building our family. Our kids needed both of us to be there for them. But, one fact lingered: we had fallen out of love. The moments of bliss, passion, closeness, intimacy, and understanding without speaking had more or less vanished. Life inside our relationship was like purgatory.

Unlike the times when we were madly in love, got married, had children, and worked at a successful joint parenting venture, we were now searching for ways to keep our marriage afloat. Strong beliefs and values, a good family, wonderful friends, and community and professional activities were not enough to keep us going.

We had come to the conclusion—at least I did—that we had to find a way to keep the children safe as we journeyed through the inevitable interpersonal difficulties that accompany the final break up. That moment came the day I returned from a foreign assignment to the U.S. After six months living away, with family visits every two or three weeks, I was advised in no uncertain terms that I had to leave.

Even though I felt it coming, I was still devastated. Hope springs eternal, doesn't it? Somehow I wished that the time away would have helped clarify the situation, bring a change of heart, or bring—more or less—a miraculous healing of our differences so everything could go back to normal. Alas, it was not to be.

So I left with my clothes and took a furnished apartment temporarily. The most difficult part was knowing that my kids needed me around but I could not be with them. The emotional pain was excruciating as I had made a vow to build a family and take care of my kids until they reached at least eighteen years old.

Carving Out my Purpose

On that sunny October day in Switzerland, I had a flash that changed my life forever. Yes, I was in great pain. Yes, I was demoralized. Yes, I wanted to escape that trap of emotional and physical anguish that messed up my whole body. I had been diagnosed with a *heart block*—me, an active, healthy, optimistic person who had never endured any illness whatsoever.

That day, God was definitely watching over me. Basking in the bright sun, I suddenly remembered why I was on earth—to make a difference! At that moment, with my eyes closed to the sun, my children appeared in my mind and reminded me that they needed a father in order to be the best they could be.

From that moment until this day, I decided to live and make a difference in the world. I committed to the well-being of my children as my top priority. It was a *deliverance* from searching, wondering, and wishing. I knew that I was the only one that could fulfill that commitment. That state of giving has pervaded everything I have done since, while building a business that helps people find their own best self through coaching.

I decided at that point to live and share my abilities, knowledge, and skills for the benefit of anyone I would work or play with. I set myself on a journey to learn how to coach others in finding their own acquired capabilities and abilities to achieve beyond their wildest expectations. And that started with my kids—guiding, coaching, assisting, and helping them be the best they could be.

The journey has been a resounding success. My oldest daughter is a professional voice artist, doing commercials and playing in live theater, and is a powerful coach in her own way, helping friends and co-workers by spreading the concepts and approaches that facilitate a productive life.

My son is the CIO of a billion-dollar company, having moved through the ranks of information technology to become a top gun in his field. I am proud to watch him ally his technical know-how to his understanding of human beings, excelling at qualities of leadership that empower and enable people to be the best at what they do. He lives the skills of goal-orientation, certainty in the workplace, opportunities for growth and contribution, and the recognition for small wins along the way.

My youngest child is most remarkable. Living as a non-binary person, gone is the confusion of many years not knowing whether she was heterosexual or gay or queer. Dealing with bipolar disorder, they have overcome alcohol and drug addiction. A teetotaler for over ten years and a certified teacher, they have worked with young girls to develop self-confidence. Their personal victories have led to podcasts and a blog dedicated to helping people afflicted by similar emotional pain. Going forward, they plan to coach people working in the field of mental illness so they may learn to apply techniques and concepts that make their work more efficient and effective.

I am forever grateful to my ex-wife for having the courage to walk away. Her decision emotionally shook me to the core and brought me to the edge; however, in living through those most difficult moments, my personal transformation took root. Her choice powered me toward the person that I could be and wanted to be. I studied and learned and developed my understanding for the benefit of so many other people, helping them through their own transformations.

I have come a long way from that mountain ledge in Switzerland. No question!

The Power of Focus and Passion

For over thirty years, I have benefitted from this moment of lucidity, of blessing in disguise. I turned my focus to being the best coach I could be and to looking for opportunities to share my experiences of transformation from despair to eternal optimism. Essentially, I turned my purpose into passion. Every day I coach someone, I deepen my conviction that we all have what it takes to succeed. I suggest that powerful self-talk sounds like *I am enough*.

Most people do not realize the power gained through their life experiences. Thus, my definition of peak performance is using *the right stuff, in the right amount, at the right time*. It behooves us to find within ourselves the one thing that drives us and makes us passionate, unbeatable, unstoppable.

You may ask: *How do I find that drive?* My answer is simple. Do an inventory of the moments in your life when you succeeded at something. Secondly, remember how you felt about that accomplishment and write it down. Thirdly, describe what you gained through this experience: confidence, self-satisfaction, a feeling of power, a feeling of *can-do*, new opportunities, recognition, a sense of belonging among others, or the joy of making a difference for others.

Seek a breakthrough transformation. Turn your purpose into passion. Learn to *know thyself*. Be the best you can be. The reward is peace of mind and a lasting optimism toward the accomplishments of your future.

Raymond Perras is a best-selling author and leadership expert, creator of Pathways to Breakthrough Transformation™. He helps people discover their inner capabilities and learn to use them consistently to achieve effort-less effectiveness. Raymond believes people can achieve anything they want once they focus and align their strengths to a clear and well-defined purpose. Success is not a fantasy; it's a formula. Learn and apply the formula. Connect with Raymond at: coachrpp@gmail.com

CHAPTER 24

Every Day a New Beginning

Shelli F. Roberts

Dawn of a New Day

When I became pregnant with my daughter, it just felt right, like it was meant to be. I loved being her mom. She was so full of life and vitality when she was young: mischievous, fun, and smart as a whip. A sensitive soul. She was a lot of things I was not—extroverted, popular, and highly social. I would have handed this little girl the moon if I could; she brought me so much joy. My heart was so full. Little did I know the war awaiting me as she grew older.

Have you ever been involved in a prolonged and perhaps traumatic situation that presented such a strong emotional challenge that all you could do was cope your way through it day by day? If I had had some of the knowledge and tools I have today, I may have been able to handle each situation better, to worry less, and to live life fully instead of being in a state of coping and victimized survival.

May I share these perspectives and tools with you so you, too, can thrive in life? They have been my greatest gift as I moved out of the darkness, along with the renewed and much healthier relationship I now have with my no-longer-little girl.

The problems started as my ex-husband came back into our lives. He was going to college and wanted to show off his daughter to his would-be wives, so he started insisting on his visitations five years after our divorce when she was three. We hadn't seen much of him before then, and having a daddy in her life was exciting and new for my girl.

As she grew into a willful preteen, he switched from lies and unfulfilled bribes to abuse, control, and criticism instead. She was growing into her own person and began to exercise her free spirit by bucking every rule he created to control her. I had primary custody, so he would call me screaming what a bad parent I was, hammering all the things I hadn't done right as a parent and spouse. He took his anger out on my daughter when she didn't conform to his vision of perfection.

His abuse was taking its toll; she would crumple in the hallway in tears right after he dropped her off from his visitation. She couldn't tell me what had happened as she *wasn't allowed* to share with me what caused her sobbing. I was heartbroken and didn't know what to do. I felt so helpless. He wouldn't say anything to me, either, when I asked. He told me nothing was going on and that he *didn't do anything*. I knew better because I had been married to the guy and subjected to the same treatment.

As my girl hit her junior high years, the situation escalated, and we had one problem after another with him: non-existent co-parenting, late or non-existent support payments, multiple court hearings, visitation ping-pong, and therapy sessions. Time and experience did not make things better as she had internalized his shame and criticism. She reached her senior year in high school and decided she was done. She tuned out both parental voices of authority and started to ignore her teachers too—she skipped school and did only the minimum amount of work for her classes.

I felt powerless and wondered if she would graduate. She coped with her anger and heartache by drinking alcohol to excess and surrounded herself with friends who did too. She started to hold *day drinks* at my house while I was at work, and then, these spilled into party weekends, every weekend. I told her I didn't want this happening in my house. She laughed and did it anyway, saying *it was her house too*.

Nothing I tried worked; she knew I wouldn't kick her out. I didn't know who she would listen to, didn't know how to reach her. I fell into deep despair and became a ghost in my own house. I held on to the vision of the beautiful, vivacious little girl I knew was still in there somewhere. I felt disempowered and like the failed parent he said I was. My daughter was treating me the same way she had been treated by her dad.

Darkness Before the Dawn

It was a month after her twenty-first birthday. She had turned her party lifestyle into a job at a nightclub. She had been abusing Adderall to stay awake all night, and finally it all caught up to her. When she was first brought to jail, I was in shock. She had experienced a mental break prompted by her lifestyle choices, and during it, she didn't know who I was. She didn't believe me when I told her I was her mother.

She refused to see me; I didn't matter to her. I have never felt so much fear for her and for *us*. What if she didn't come back from this? Could I still love this person I didn't know anymore? I fought further despair but decided I was *not* helpless in this situation. I worked with the system to get her transferred to the state mental facility that could help her recover.

The staff told me she would get back to a more normal level of mental functioning but couldn't say anything about the person who would emerge when her brain chemicals were brought back into balance. Throughout her recovery, I held on to the hope that the beautiful person I knew beneath all the pain would step forward.

I visited every weekend and got glimpses into her progress. I stayed in touch with the staff and felt blessed she was in good hands. I worked with the system to address her charges, one of which was a felony that could keep her jailed after her recovery for up to five years. Finally, five months later, the mental facility released her for trial, and the judge ruled that she could come home.

Breaking of a New Day

I looked around the cold and impersonal white walls of the police holding facility as I waited for my daughter to be out-processed. I felt excited that she was coming home and also faint optimism that this experience might catalyze a change in her choices and lifestyle. I wasn't completely sure how *back to normal* she was and worried about the possibility of lingering mental health issues that would need continuing treatment or monitoring. I was in completely new territory, another scary unknown. I did know that I would be standing strong for her as she rebuilt her life.

It was 11:00 at night when the county police finally released my daughter back into my custody. I had been at the station all day, rehashing everything that had happened to bring us to that point. I was exhausted and embattled. And hopeful. I resolved that this experience would not be wasted. And, it would not be repeated. This needed to be the breaking point of a pattern that *could not* continue.

She finally emerged from the back of the facility. I felt joy to be reunited and to have her know me. I was relieved that she was grateful I was there for her, to take her home. I asked her what she wanted the most right at that moment. As I fulfilled her desire for a juicy steakburger, I resolved that this would be the first day of the rest of our lives.

Every Day a New Beginning

I didn't have a support network in my journey through darkness—or many other resources either. One of the hardest things to do through my despair was to see any hope for better possibilities. I was shut down and victimized, until I discovered these practices that brought me from surviving to thriving.

I share these tools with you for the times you, too, are struggling through despair:

- Set the tone for your day because how you start your day is also how it unfolds. Create a morning ritual. When I was waking up each day with dread, I chose self-care. I exercised, walked outside, listened to upbeat music, and meditated.
- Recognize and honor how you feel. You are not powerless, even if it feels like it. Know that it is okay to feel the way you do, but also know it is a choice to hold on to disempowering emotions, such as worry or anger. Feel your feelings and then move on.
- Take deep cleansing breaths. Choose your reactions. As my ex was screaming at me on the phone, I chose not to buy in to what he was accusing me of. In moments of crisis, ask yourself: What is the most empowering thing you can think, do, or say that honors yourself and your values?
- Shift your focus because what you focus on grows. Are your thoughts disempowering? Judgmental? Blaming? If so, these situations are what you are inviting into your experience. What would you like to experience instead? Focus on that.

Know that every day is a new beginning and you are the creator of your reality. Our lives are crafted moment by moment and by how we interact with them. Choose to make them beautiful!

Shelli F. Roberts has a strong spiritual background and loves nurturing others, guiding her clients in their own self-empowerment journeys, and being a part of her daughter's life. After a lifetime of bullying and narcissistic abuse, she has healed from her traumas and holds a great deal of compassion for those who are still recovering from theirs. She has a master's degree, multiple certifications, and practices shamanic energy healing. Connect with Shelli at: joyfultransformation.life/contact-us

CHAPTER 25

The Words Leapt Off the Page

Sue Salvemini

I remember it like it was yesterday. It was the end of January 2016, and I was sitting at my kitchen table, my back to the double glass doors that overlooked our back yard. The warm morning sun was gently rising behind me, shining radiant light around my arms and into the room. With my study Bible propped wide open to my left and my journal beneath my right hand, I quickly scribbled my thoughts, trying to catch up to my brain.

Why do I have such horrifically illegible handwriting? I thought as I observed my white knuckled grip on my pen, my fingers too close to the tip. *Slow down*, I thought, *and breathe. The thoughts will not escape you. Take your time, write so you can actually read your thoughts, and capture it all. You will not lose the words.*

I paused and took a long, welcomed sip from my morning coffee—hot with just enough cream from my favorite white Gevalia Coffee *gift with purchase* porcelain mug. My mother and I always joked about this mug having the perfectly sized "thin-lip, like pure china" she would say, making the coffee taste "especially good." *I miss her. Gosh, do I really, really miss her.*

My mind wandered. It had been five years since she died, and not a day went by that I didn't achingly miss her and smile, thinking about her all in the same nanosecond. Other than my husband, she was my closest friend and someone I could always talk to about anything. I wondered: if she were here, what she would be saying about the past five years? The house we built after the house fire? Would she love this kitchen like I do? She was integral to the design, unbeknownst to her.

I glanced at the front door ahead of me and saw the glass motif that she picked out while lying beside me in her bed. When her earthly life was approaching an end, I had lain with her, designing this very kitchen, part of our new earthly home being born. The irony never escaped me. I imagined how she would have consoled me during my unexpected and devastating job loss from a company I was so passionately committed to. I smiled, knowing her wisdom—*when one door closes, many more open*—helped guide me from anguish to growth and opportunity, blessing me with my recent three-year job leading a small startup company that was now closing due to an acquisition.

As I sat in my kitchen, I was contemplating the next part of my journey, as I was without a job for the first time in my life. I glanced back at my Bible and continued to pray. I had been doing this daily for the entire month of January, from the same chair in my kitchen, after the kids were off to school and my husband was at work, teaching and inspiring third graders. This was my time of silence and reflection, a newly established, non-negotiable commitment to start every day moving forward in study and prayer.

I prayed:

Lord, for years I have sought your guidance. I sit in church on Sundays, committed to following you. Yet I return to my days and go about business as usual. Today, Jesus, I feel ready. How do you want to use me? It is time, God, for me to truly trust you for guidance, not just in thoughts, but in action—in all areas of my life, including work. I am prepared to be faithful and fearless and do your work. Show me your will, and then give me the ears to hear, the heart to know, and the strength to take action.

Pausing, I looked down at my journal. Staring at me were circled words and lines—a word jumble of sorts that closely resembled the tinker toys and model molecules I once played with as a child. Words I'd added daily included headers, such as Strengths, Gifts, Passions, Love to Dos, Hate to Dos, Good Ats, Bad Ats, Easy, Hard, Ideal Week, Month—to name a few.

Beneath each category were words, such as faith, family, speaking, teaching, leadership, people, love, fun, sales, coaching, teams, development, impact, inspiration, writing, business, travel—so many words, jumbled on the pages in front of me with no pattern, sequence, or logical sense. All these words were staring at me, some illegible even to my eyes, clearly written with a rush like water exploding out of a fire hose. I stared at them. I prayed over them. And I quietly sat, feeling the warmth of the sun rising even higher on my back.

And then, I had a turning point like never before.

My heart rate picked up. The words, once jumbled, leapt off the page and found order, forming three distinct pillars. I felt an intense warm embrace and a rush of tears—uncontrollable, overwhelming tears. I gasped, trying to catch my breath. I looked up from my journal and saw the particles of dust dancing in the rays from the sun, landing on the table in front of me.

I heard a voice, not my own, say, "Leadership, training, develop, inspire."

"Me?" I asked. "On my own, or with others?"

"You. Trust me; this is where I want you."

This message was crystal clear to me. I was terrified and relieved in one breath. "With who? How?" I prayed. "Leaders? Corporate? Non corporate? Christians? Who, Jesus, who?!"

"Go into your space. Go be in this world. Go to businesses. I will bring you the people. I have been preparing you for this for a long time. Go use the gifts I gave you and don't look back. They are staring at you on the pages before you. Just trust in me. I have you."

After the sobbing stopped, I dried my face and got working. I had no idea how this would happen, nor did I know how I would replace a significant six figure income—income that was a critical contribution to our earthly livelihood. The message from God, Jesus, the Holy Spirit—three-in-one—was tattooed on my heart and soul, and my company, Focal Pointe, was launched three months later.

So what changed?

This turning point moment was me choosing to turn *every* aspect of my life over to God, including my professional career, finances, marriage, and family. And this time, I *was* ready. And I haven't looked back. Prior to this moment, I *felt* as if I was giving it all to God, but in reality, I relied heavily on my own efforts.

I was proud of my ability to work relentlessly, multitask, and juggle family, work, fun, service—you name it! I was proud of the results I obtained. I was thankful that God equipped me with a beautiful family, stamina, a strong work ethic, a love for people, and a passion for leadership. I was thankful for my upbringing and the countless blessings in my life. And while I believed God was intertwined with all of it, I didn't fully understand what it meant to abandon self and ego and to truly seek and follow His lead in every way, faithfully and fearlessly.

It has now been just over seven years since I started my executive coaching and leadership development business, and I can share that not a single day has gone by that I haven't pinched myself and said, "I love my job. I love my clients. I am doing exactly what I was created to be doing."

Every aspect of this journey has been filled with blessings. And while I have felt joyful for most of my life, the greatest change I have experienced is a new level of inner peace and harmony. I still work hard; however, it is work guided by my creator—for Him and to glorify Him. My inner drive and work ethic, once fueled by my own pride, has been replaced by something much greater. The result is ease and calmness and peace in my days. I have a faith that has replaced any fear about decisions and choices, allowing me to truly embrace moments and experiences with those I care so deeply about: my family, friends, and colleagues.

Watching my clients achieve the same peace is my greatest reward. I want everyone I meet to have days filled with *pinch me* moments: days that are completely aligned with their God-given uniqueness and exclusive combination of gifts, working and living in alignment with their core values and purpose. I want this for my clients, and I want this for *you.*

The first step in this journey is to truly connect with your creator and embrace your unique talents and gifts. I invite you to take some time in prayer, reflection, and meditation. Grab what's in your heart. Write it down. Let the words hang on the paper, and see what you discover. Start with categories as I outlined and see what God reveals to you. Please, share them with me. You might just find it becomes *your* Turning Point Moment, as it did for me!

Sue Salvemini, MEd, CPC, PCC, is an author, speaker, and executive leadership coach, helping leaders align their work with their core values for maximum impact and personal fulfillment. In her book, *Leadership by Choice,* Sue guides readers through a journey of reflection exercises, applying over twenty-five years of best practices from her experiences in the military, in the corporate world, and through supporting executive clients. For support uncovering your *Turning Point* moments, connect with Sue and access complimentary resources/guides at: www.focalpointeinc.com

CHAPTER 26

The Power of Perseverance

Tom Salvemini

The plane rattled and shook as I felt more than heard the thump of my heart over the plane's grumbling engine. A small personal challenge, this was to be the first thing I crossed off my newly-formed bucket list. I sat, surprisingly calm, strapped to my instructor in what can only be described as a Baby Björn for adults. Soon enough, he tapped me on the shoulder, and we crab-walked to the open doorway. This was it—no backing out, only one way down. As I looked down at the miniature world below, my first thought was that we might fall out, and my second thought was, *You fool, that's exactly what's supposed to happen.*

Another shoulder tap and in the next moment, we tumbled into the mid-morning sky, and I caught a brief glimpse of the belly of the departing plane. As we dropped like a rock from the sky, the uprush of wind felt a bit like a pillow of air. When the chute opened and the excitement ebbed, I couldn't help but think about what had brought me to this moment.

So why am I jumping out of a plane when I don't tolerate heights of any kind? Oddly enough, it started in my third grade classroom. For me, family aside, there was no greater joy than working with my third graders. I held my students to high expectations while at the same time using interactive, hands-on activities to motivate their learning. In return, they worked incredibly hard for me, and we enjoyed many fun lessons and activities together. Teaching my students *how* to think, rather than *what* to think, was always the cornerstone of my teaching style.

Every year, I taught my students about the virtue of perseverance. As with teaching other virtues, such as honesty, humility, and empathy, I brought in guest speakers to talk about how one of these virtues guided both their personal life and their career. Unexpectedly, one day the lesson came home to me.

When teaching any lesson, it's important to begin with an anticipatory set, or something that hooks the interest of the students. For this lesson on perseverance, I started by describing my friend David. I shared with the kids that my friend was an elementary teacher just like me, and a scuba diver just like me. I told the kids he was also sky diver and a rugby player. He had been on a big cat safari in Africa, and he wrote for travel magazines. Finally, being the owner of a used minivan, I begrudgingly told the kids that he also drove a Maserati, maybe one of the coolest cars ever. As usual, hearing about David's active life always excited the kids, and this year was no different.

Finally, David's visit rolled around on a Friday afternoon. A long week of work behind them, my students talked quietly on the carpet in front of me. *This will be a lesson they'll never forget,* I once again thought to myself. I'd seen this experience play out many times over the years, but I guess I had never really listened to the message David had to share.

I knew his talk inside and out, or so I thought. Why this visit was different I cannot say, but that afternoon his visit took root in me and started me on my own long overdue journey.

When David, a quadriplegic since the age of eighteen, finally arrived and rolled through our classroom door in his custom wheelchair, the reaction was always the same: first, stunned silence and confused looks, then inquisitive questions, and finally a deeper understanding of David and what it means to persevere in life. Over the course of an hour, David warmly touched their lives as he talked about his condition, how he navigated daily activities, and how he believed perseverance allowed him to live an active, full life.

That day, as I sat passively listening to David, he shared his belief about the value and importance of persevering in life. On one level, I was hearing many of the details I had heard in previous visits, but on some other level, I was hearing it in a completely different way. It seemed like David was directly talking to me. The room seemed to melt away until it was just the two of us. My inner voice blocked out all else as a personal conversation unfolded inside my head.

I always told my third graders they could achieve anything they put their minds to. I asked myself: *Am I really living and modeling that belief? Do I have perseverance and the confidence in myself to do some of the things on my ill-formed bucket list, things that will both intimidate and challenge me?* I had always wanted to try sky diving, despite having a healthy fear of heights and roller coaster drops. I had always loved the thrill and freedom of flying and had hopes of getting my private pilot's license. I'd wanted to do this for a long time, and a pilot friend of mine encouraged me to pursue my license every time he took me flying.

In the background, David was answering questions from the students while thoughts and questions swirled in my mind. *Is getting my private pilot's license a possibility?* I asked myself again. Yes, planes and skydiving were possibilities, but the big one, the item at the top of my list, was the desire to write children's books. *Why have I never really pursued this?*

As David talked, I marveled at all my friend had done and accomplished in his life despite being in a wheelchair, not having the use of his legs, and only slight use of one arm. It sounds every bit the cliché, but in that moment, it really was as if a switch had been thrown in my psyche.

During that talk, I realized many of my dreams in life had been locked in a self-imposed state of inertia—partly because my focus had always been on my family and my teaching career, but more so due to my lack of confidence. So what happened during his visit? I can't say for sure, but I certainly felt the seismic shift that took place. I know it was David's words as well as his inspirational example, but why his message hit home that day, when I had heard it for years, I can't explain.

In part, I think David's influence was wrapped up in my own guilt of knowing a person with so many challenges was not deterred and had many more life experiences than me. Quite frankly, he had done things I had only talked about. But it was also the realization that life was passing me by, and I had let some of the things I had hoped to accomplish in life go untended. It's funny how fast time passes, and all things you say you'll get around to often just slip away.

Sometimes a deeper understanding of ourselves doesn't come so easily, and some of the lessons life has for us have to be learned the hard way. Why is that? I really believe many of us battle our own inner-voice of self-doubt on a daily basis. For me, I was often paralyzed by the overwhelming fear of failure. If I couldn't excel at something, then I just didn't attempt it. I took the safer and easier way out. As you can guess, I missed out on a lot of great experiences. As for writing children's books, I often thought I'd do it someday, but *someday* never came. This realization became my turning point.

I took a year's leave of absence from my teaching position, did some research by talking to local artists and authors, and spent a few months completing drafts of my first three books. My first book, *Band of Gorillas*, is in publication, and the second, *Conceivable*—a tribute to David—is awaiting artwork. I can't say it was an easy process or that I didn't make a few mistakes along the way, but I plowed ahead, determined to see a children's book through to publication.

We all need to understand that someday is really today. So, what is it you've been thinking about doing? Just know the thought of doing something challenging is often far worse than actually doing it. Choose one thing and go after it. Don't let fear, or the fear of failure, stop you.

After most visits, I would walk with David as he rolled out to his car parked in the handicapped space next to a used gray minivan. Winking, I would always say, "Stop parking in this spot. You, my friend, are not handicapped!"

Sometimes the only thing stopping us is our unwillingness to try. I understand now that we are all handicapped to a small degree, but it never stopped David. Now, it doesn't stop me. Is it stopping you?

Tom Salvemini was blessed to be an elementary teacher for twenty-five years, supporting hundreds of students and families. He is most proud of his exceptional wife and three beautiful children. While he continues to write children's books, he also loves to scuba dive, exercise, travel, and restore vintage pinball machines. You can connect with Tom at salveminitom@gmail.com or learn more about his work at www.tomsalvemini.com

CHAPTER 27

Your Path to Light

Omar Sánchez

The light was usually with me in my life. Since I was a young child, it gave me the energy to run fast from one way to another. When my father called to me, I ran to see him. After he gave me an order, I went out to run errands. I had infinite energy.

I also loved to talk with my parents for hours when we were on vacations. Because I love to have conversations, I entered a Toastmaster's Club as an adult. I love to talk with people and make new friends every day.

Have you ever had an extreme or hard situation in your life that you didn't know how to get through? Come along with me to examine my serious situation, and perhaps you will see how the path of the light can help you.

After the end of the influenza health crisis in 2009 in Mexico, I was working as a partner in a small company with two friends. I was happy, independent, and finding my own way in the life. I did my sales work, visiting hotels that purchased our wood for maintenance purposes. I played every day with my three-year-old little daughter, and that made me feel like the happiest father in the world. I was living in the bright side of life.

However, my father lived in the general darkness, and I kept my distance from him. Until that fated day in 2010.

I had received a loan from the bank, and I lent it to my father to help him in his business. His darkness was growing more and more in those days, and mine was growing, too—without me knowing it. I had asked for the money back from my father without success on several occasions. So one day, I decided to go see him at his office in the lumberyard, and my wife accompanied me.

I felt anger dominating me on the way to the office. At that time, I didn't know how to control that feeling. Anger was a sensation that began in my forearms, then moved to my jaw, and on to my brain. It made me feel anxious, impatient, and just bad in general. I was one step away from exploding against anything or anyone. So, I shouldn't have gone to see anyone in that condition.

But I did go. We arrived at the store counter, and my dad made us go to his office. The conversation was fine until he said he was not going to pay me. My wife intervened in that moment, and a fight with words began. My dad disrespected her, and I had to intervene to defend her. Soon the discussion was out of control.

We screamed at each other, and then I felt an overflowing anger in response to his behavior toward my wife and me. I suddenly threw a big plastic object and hit his head, which opened a wound on his eyebrow that began to bleed. It was like a nightmare scene—frightening and horrific. Then my dad took a letter opener, held it like a dagger, and prepared to attack me.

Fortunately by this point, my mother had come down from the upper office, and all the employees had come to the office to see what was happening. My wife and I left my father's lumberyard to avoid a worse tragedy. This was the most tremendous turning point of my life. At that moment, I hit rock bottom within the dark side of myself.

At that moment, I felt guilty and extremely disturbed, so my wife calmed me down with her kindness and wisdom. Afterward, I decided to go to acupuncture therapy with a professional friend we have known for years. I saw him several times and progressively felt better. But this was only the beginning of my personal transformation to come back to the light.

Shortly after this incident, my dearest friend Jorge invited me to a Buddhist group. The leader of this group warned me that I was going to see and hear strange things, but it was good. Everyone present in the place (a particular house) was given a little book. We spoke an unusual pray in Japanese called Gongyo (assiduous prayer). After this activity, we met to learn about Buddism, followed by a session of questions and answers. Buddism helped me a lot as I repaired myself into a new and better person. During this period of time, I saw amazing views and landscapes in my dreams as part of my healing process.

My wife also helped me a lot because she recommended a magnificent book of metaphysics called *Metaphysics 4 in 1* by Florence Schovel Schinn (Prana 2019, reprinted).

This series of books talks about the power of positive thinking among other things. If we think good things, we are going to receive good things in our life. But watch out! If we have negative thoughts in our life, we are going to have negative things in our life. People think we can play with words however we want without consequences, but that is not true. The world needs positive phrases everywhere, especially in public places, like bus stations, airports, shopping malls, etc.

The books of Florence Schovel were written early in the twentieth century, and we are just now seeing some positive phrases in restaurants, shops, and in various enterprises. I think this shift is the beginning of the path of light on Earth. It's a start.

In this period of time, I didn't have a car, even though I had a small company that sold wood and forest products to the big hotels in Cancun and Rivera Maya in the Mexican state of Quintana Roo. So I had to walk a lot to visit my clients: to enter or exit from the hotels.

It is a long way between the security entrance and the maintenance buildings or purchasing offices. Thankfully, this kind of walking kept me in shape.

I was lucky that my parents didn't report me to the authorities after the incident with my father in his lumberyard. I felt guilty, and I wanted to make peace with my dad.

Several months later, I made peace with my father. He was leaving a bank near my house, and I arrived at that place at the same moment. I gave him a sincere apology, and he accepted it, telling me that he also wanted to be fine with me. At the end of everything, we were son and father again. We were good friends from that time until he died, giving me longed-for peace. We both moved on in life.

How did I get through these circumstances?

- Through the teachings of Buddhism
- Going to sessions of periodic acupuncture
- Through forgiving and making amends with the person I fought horribly (in my case, my father)
- Reading books about metaphysics (in my case, four) and repeating positive phrases most of the time
- Getting a lot of exercise (every day, delivering my wood orders)
- Listening to my wife's advice

These are the practices that helped me understand that I couldn't be the same person I was before the attack on my father. I had to be a better person and look for all the necessary help I needed. I learned that the world was bigger than I thought in the past. I saw things at a distance, as if I was looking through a telescope. The negativity had taken over me, and I didn't understand the effects, like a lot of people in the world.

We all think that we are fine—that we think, feel, and do things in the correct way. We often don't know that we have fallen into the dark side until it's too late. So be careful. Like Master Yoda teaches in *Star Wars*: fear, anger, and aggressiveness represent the dark side. If we allow them to rule our lives, they will control our destiny forever.

In this present time, I try to follow this advice in order to be a good and better person every day.

If you have difficult problems to solve in your life, I hope you can learn from the things that happened to me as I grew to be a resilient person: a human who learns to face problems, to become stronger, and to keep moving in life. Follow the advice I give you or seek advice from your friends, family, or professionals who really love and appreciate you.

Remember that you are the creator of your own life, and life is beautiful. Follow your path to light.

Omar Sánchez Estrella has a degree in business administration from La Salle University and studied metaphysics in the books of Florence Shovel Shinn. He also studied healing humanism for several years. Omar worked as a salesman for over twenty-five years. He is competent leader and trained communicator with Toastmasters International. He likes to write and help people grow to be better persons. Connect with Omar at: exitomadera@gmail.com

CHAPTER 28

A Life-Changing Visit

Camille Titone

It was another exhausting day at the inpatient locked psychiatric ward. Down a long, darkened corridor sat a plump man on a red sofa. He was of Indian descent. Prior to seeing him, I sensed his presence. I heard barely a whisper of my name, so I looked down the darkened hallway and saw his left arm extended, his index finger beckoning me to join him. Without hesitation, I walked toward him, thinking him a doctor.

He wore a white polyester, 1970s-styled John Travolta suit that reminded me of the movie, *Saturday Night Fever*. Glancing down, I silently chuckled because he wore shiny, white patent leather low-cut boots. Suddenly I wondered: *Is this guy for real?* Immediately, in his presence, I felt peace and tranquility. Even though there was plenty of room to join him on the sofa, I knew to kneel in front of this mysterious man. Then, I sat crossed-legged.

He began to speak. His voice was soft and gentle. I felt overwhelmingly happy, suddenly appreciative. He questioned, "I understand you do not wish to take your medication?"

I responded, "No, I don't!"

He smiled. Surprisingly, he was aware of my experience from the month prior to this encounter. This doctor knew of the sweet feminine voice who whispered in my left ear, guiding me through a difficult circumstance. He began to ask deeper questions about the beautiful, graceful voice I heard pre- and post-sleep.

We conversed for what seemed a lengthy time. Finally he said, "I must go, but I want you to know you are experiencing a Sanskrit word, known as *samadhi*."

I answered, "Oh, okay!" not fully understanding its significance. Politely I nodded and walked toward the direction of my room. Happy, I skipped down the hallway. I turned back around to wave goodbye, but he was gone. The next morning, I discovered *John Travolta* wouldn't have had an exit route without walking with me toward my room the day before.

Prior to this hospitalization, I spent evenings at my altar as this lyrical voice consoled me. She eased the nervousness from my keenly troubled mind. One Sunday night, exhausted during the eight o'clock hour, I suddenly heard her. She chimed, "Oh, that is such old news," and giggled.

The hospital rooms in the ward were filled with people in dis-ease; nonetheless, many of these people became friends for a short time. After nine days in the ward, I was released early on the Eve of Christmas. Upon my arrival on the ward, once coherent, I had been receiving and making calls along with the other patients standing in line using a public phone. This phone was our only connection to the outside world.

Knowing how strongly I felt about medication, my closest friends, Lyn and Peg urged me, "Just take the pills, Camille!"

Defiantly, I would not give in. I knew in my soul that nothing during this episode was wrong. I thought I didn't need the *meds* as long as *her* guidance was with me. The pressure, intense from friends, family, and staff, wore me down. And, there was a strict rule: *No one leaves without accepting the medication.*

After seeing the Indian doctor, I finally relented, realizing staying in the hospital indefinitely wasn't a good option. The duty nurse always watched me *swallow* as part of their protocol.

Alone, I welcomed the enclosed small closet space to pray and did my best to meditate, calling for her sweet voice's guidance. Her laugher let me know this hospitalization was not a huge deal. She said, "You'll look back and find this amusing and meaningful one day."

Now, I see the humor and the purpose of her visits. A lot of time was spent in the safe oasis—away from everyone—in the farthest point at the back of my closet in the ward. I recall sitting in there, crying vehemently.

As the psychotropic drugs took effect, her voice did return, only it slowly turned into a male, garbled voice. Reverberating slowly in my ear, I heard the last words ever during this unique blissful contact: "You're a soul to be reckoned with!"

At the exit interview with my parents and hospital staff to discuss my next steps, I scanned the room of circular chairs set up. Asking, "Where is the Indian doctor? Isn't he going to join us?" I was told, "There is no Indian doctor on staff."

Stunned, I wondered: *Who was that?* Today, I know he was a Guide, sent to allow me to relent. When I needed guidance most, Spirit came through.

I was grateful to be home in my familiar surroundings; however, there was now loneliness without her coddling, blessings, and kind words of encouragement. No longer did she grace me with her repertoire, faithfully lulling me with conversation. At times, I felt *they* numbed my heart, soul, and mind. Yet honestly, I have hope, faith, and trust that she will return, which fills my heart, allowing me to choose to live on.

The Life Changing Visit of *Them*

My journey in the late 1980s—during my twenties—had begun to fortify by 1990. On an unconscious level, I had known since birth that I was meant to complete a life's mission.

In my youth and throughout my life, I have reverently loved God, Our Father, and Jesus. One summer, I chose each day to sit cross-legged in the farthest corner of my bedroom, singing "I Believe" and "Let There Be Peace on Earth." The emphasis, I am now certain, was on the part of the song asking for peace to begin *within* me. I miraculously sprouted a higher vibrational energy.

Did you ever reach a higher vibrational level at junctures in your timeline, fortifying a realization of a supreme understanding of who and why you are here and your life's purpose? Unconsciously, at nine years old, I already knew mine. Consistently, I devoted much time to quietude. Although deep traumas occurred, I never lost sight of this dream nor my love for my two best friends.

Another huge growth period for me was in the eighties. Returning from Holy Communion one Sunday Mass in silence and gratitude, I listened to "I, the Sky." I felt the devotion of encasing The Holy Eucharist in my heart in its purity. I won't soon forget the opening of my heart chakra that day. As the community sang at Mass and music filled my ears, the song spoke of my wish to hold God's people in my heart.

Suddenly, I developed a warm glow. Next, a burning fire overflowed from inside. Emphatically I stated, "Oh, yes God! I *will* hold *all your people always*." I felt completion and smiled as I knelt in my pew. Again, I received the key message of my life's mission. However, at that time, I was clueless of our gift of chakras. And life again desensitized this magnificent moment. I moved on in my daily life without much thought to this exquisite experience.

In 1988, lower back surgery beset me—six intense hours. My orthopedic surgeon told me he'd wished a neurosurgeon had been present. A bundle of nerves lay caught in the solid mass of a closed disc. Constructively chiseling its solid center, the doctor told me to never have spinal surgery again. To date in 2023, I've had three surgeries. After the surgery, a series of events unraveled my whole life thus far. My brain slowed to still pictures. I asked: *Who am I?* I realized I was an incarnation of Christ, sent to serve the world.

Depleted of energy, I remained awake most nights running this scenario in my mind with a vengeance. For the next nineteen months, my secret snowballed. I prayed to be let go from a position I could no longer function in. Months passed, and I could not add one plus one, remembering it equaled two. I felt if I was to be Christ in the world, I radically needed transformation to become a perfect soul.

Currently in 2023, I've experienced mornings where both my ears breathe and pulse. At times, undistinguishable voices in whispers of banter occur all at once, and it's difficult to make sense of any. My mentor and spiritual coach suggested I ask them, "Please slow down so I can audibly sense what you are stating."

I know the Sanskrit language from the Bronze Age. S*amadhi* means "communication with a higher power or being." In our Golden Age, I will laugh at my 2003 experience. My encounter with *John Travolta,* pseudo doctor, allowed me freedom and conscious clues to absolutely know I am advancing in psychic abilities.

The gift of a supreme voice from Above is enough to know you are loved. However, confusion can easily set in when the mental realm wins over God's grace. Remember that finding mental wellness in the experience of illness requires patience and compassion from those in your circle and from yourself as well.

Camille Titone is a leader and visionary. She had a late beginning, as early in life her psychic abilities were shut down. She continues to become more aware and conscious. Her first and foremost joy is spirituality. Camille's first book is due out at the end of 2023. She hopes this story inspires you to read her debut book. You can email her at: sanddollar.expressions@gmail.com

CHAPTER 29

Making Things Better

Dr. Jo Ann Tober

I grew up in a small industrial town in a very traditional family. My grandparents had immigrated to North America for a better life and instilled in the family the importance of hard work and an education. My parents left school early to help support their families and were always careful and frugal with money. Working hard and getting good grades were expected. This led to me striving for perfection and not being satisfied by less.

I distinctly remember events, such as getting an excellent report card or doing well on a test, and the ensuing discussion focusing—not on the positive—but on what I had gotten wrong to ensure it didn't happen again. It wasn't until much later in life that I realized just how firmly I had adopted the values of hard work, education, and frugality.

It was expected that I would go to university but not for a career, such as medicine or law, but to get a degree before I got married. I completed a bachelor's degree in nursing, a good choice for a woman—something I could always do part-time when married with a family.

Nursing did appeal to me on several levels. I was attracted to the study of science and the medical aspects of the training, as well as the compassionate, caring side of the profession. I saw caring for people when they were most vulnerable as an important responsibility. I was on a trajectory to be a caring professional, a wife and mother, and a perfectionist.

After graduation, I obtained a full-time position as a public health nurse (PHN) in a public health department. The field of health promotion and disease prevention appealed to me as I wanted to intervene early to prevent illness and suffering. I taught prenatal classes, visited families with new babies, taught classes in schools, and immunized children. I loved the variety and working with people of all ages.

I had been trained in my nursing program to follow a problem-solving approach, seek out knowledge, constantly evaluate my practice, and make evidence-informed decisions. I was eager to put my schooling into practice. I worked in public health for three years, working with my PHN colleagues in preschool health clinics every spring. The purpose of these clinics was to screen children before school entry to identify issues with vision, hearing, or development.

I noticed that no issues were being identified. I presented my supervisor with a proposal to conduct a program evaluation. She agreed and the evaluation was completed. The data did confirm that although significant time and staffing went into these clinics, vision, hearing, or developmental issues were not being identified. My supervisor reviewed the results of the evaluation and then followed up with me to let me know that the program would continue with no changes. She indicated that the program had been ongoing for a long time, they liked it the way it was, and so it would continue unchanged. "That was the way we have always done it," I believe was the actual comment. An expression which I despise to this day.

What? This made no sense to me. I can now concede that there may have been other factors impacting the decision that were outside of my understanding, but at the time, I was young and idealistic. Why would evidence and data from the evaluation be ignored? Why would resources continue to be directed to an ineffective program? I would have been satisfied with any type of response, such as reviewing the assessment tools or investigating the timing of the assessments. I found the complete lack of action disheartening and discouraging. The decision to reform the program was not mine to make, so I did my job and tried to ignore the seemingly inefficient approach.

I had been a happy frontline nurse. I was no longer very happy. Evidence was not being used to support decisions, and I was practicing in an environment that was at odds with my values. This experience motivated me to want to complete a master's degree to be able to obtain skills, credibility, and a position with the authority to be able to effect change.

My reaction to this experience was about to launch a series of events that dramatically changed the trajectory of my life.

My husband and I had previously discussed my completing a master's degree. When I brought up the idea, he agreed, but with little enthusiasm. He was willing to allow me to complete the degree on the condition that it did not impact his life—not exactly an overwhelming level of support. I agreed and applied for a master's program at the local university.

I received a polite letter informing me that I had not been accepted into the program. My immediate response was, *Oh, well, that is that*. I have always been a humble person and figured that I just wasn't good enough for a post-graduate degree. When I informed a friend, she encouraged me to follow up to receive feedback so that I would at least understand why.

I hesitated, then figured, *Why not?* It would be useful to know, and then I could put thoughts of a master's to rest. I did follow up and had a meeting with the head of the program who reviewed my application. He indicated that my application was indeed strong. He offered me a part-time position in the program on the spot and followed up about a full-time position, which I was subsequently offered.

Starting the master's program led to new challenges and insecurities. I was surrounded by people who seemed confident and knew exactly what they wanted to do. I was still trying to figure that out. I took courses that were far out of my previous experience, so I fell back on my problem-solving skills and sought out resources to figure out the material. Failure was not an option in my perfectionist mindset.

During my time in the program, a new PhD program was started, and I was encouraged to continue my studies and to complete a PhD. I discussed this with my husband, who forbid it. After struggling with the decision for months—in retrospect, probably years—we divorced. Surprisingly, this wasn't a shock to my friends.

I worked part-time, taught at the university, and went on to complete a PhD over the next four years. Near the completion of my PhD, I returned to public health in a senior leadership position and ultimately became a chief executive officer (CEO).

Returning to school gave me confidence, which allowed me to accomplish things I had never even considered. The more I learned, the more I appreciated how little I knew and how much there was to learn.

I realized the importance of operating with integrity and staying true to my values. I also learned the meaning of the expression, *the courage of convictions,* and that there are costs to staying true to oneself.

I valued input from others and different perspectives. Without these opinions, I would never have returned to school to complete either a master's or a PhD.

There were many barriers to overcome that required perseverance and determination. Overcoming challenges led to developing grit, resilience, and resistance to intimidation. The grit and resilience I developed were essential when I returned to public health—where many challenges continued, including harassment and bullying as I was a nurse and a woman in a still predominantly male-dominated leadership system and a physician-dominated health care system. I have continued to learn and grow in many ways, including embracing positive psychology and actively seeking out coping strategies to deal with burnout.

Here are a few lessons I learned along the way. I hope they help you in your journey:

1. Always continue to learn and grow. Use data and evidence and be open to change. If you are going to do something, do it to the best of your ability.
2. It is important to do the right thing, to act with integrity. Challenge the system. If you know something isn't working, question it and change it to make it better. How much farther ahead would we be if everyone made the improvements they could?
3. Seek support. Without encouragement, I would not have followed up about graduate school, completed my education, or pursued the career that I did.
4. Ask for input and the opinions of others. The perspectives of others can change the way you view a situation or even yourself
5. Be persistent. There are always barriers and challenges, but they can be overcome. If you can't go around a barrier, go over it. Search until you find the way.

Never stop working to make things better.

Jo Ann Tober is a registered nurse with a BScN, an MSc in Health Behavior, and a PhD in Applied Health Sciences. She holds certificates in community health nursing and positive psychology and remains a passionate advocate for evidence-informed practice, perseverance, being adaptable, challenging the status quo, and staying humble. Jo Ann lives in Southern Ontario where she enjoys antiquing with her husband, agility training with her border collies, reading novels, and anything chocolate. Jo Ann can be reached at: NeverStopActingWithIntegrity@gmail.com.

CHAPTER 30

The Gift of Giving

Dr. Tanya Wulff

I was three years old. Hovering over me, I could see the nurses' starched white caps, like birds' wings ready to fly. One of the nurses said, "You can have ice cream."

I sat up, coughing and vomiting blood, which a nurse deftly caught in a metal kidney basin under my chin. They were very kind, but all I could do was cry. My parents were still at home, my tonsils were gone, and my throat was burning.

This is my earliest memory of contact with helping professions. I was in distress, and the nurses were there to comfort me. And the ice cream did help!

I did not remember seeing the doctor at the hospital when he removed my tonsils. Months later, my parents noted that the sore throats and constant ear infections I had suffered prior to the tonsillectomy were gone. Not only was I sleeping better, but my mother was no longer up at night distressed by a crying child with earaches.

Over time, I forgot the discomfort of the surgery and decided I wanted to be able to help children the way I had been helped. When I was five and attending school, life provided an experience that set me firmly on my path.

My mother was entertaining one of her friends from the local Women's Institute, serving tea and cookies. The lady politely asked me, "And what do you want to be when you grow up?"

"A doctor," I replied.

"You mean a nurse, dear," she smiled. I did not reply, knowing my mother would label such behavior as talking back to her guest; in those days, children were seen and not heard.

The woman's comment was understandable. In the 1950s, most Canadian doctors were men. I might have chosen to become a nurse had I been a more obedient child, bent on listening to my elders. However, I was not. Have I mentioned that I was a stubborn child? Telling me I could not do something sparked in me a burning desire to do that very thing. And while the nurses were comforting, it was the doctor who had removed my tonsils and cured the earaches. I resolved to become a doctor.

I began reading books about science in bed at night, under the covers, fascinated by what I was learning. Scientific curiosity led to more events that totally frustrated my mother. I slipped into a ditch full of dirty water, ruining my new Easter coat while attempting to collect tadpoles in a mason jar. I lost my boots in the mud while inspecting garter snakes and interesting bugs that could walk on water. My collecting various caterpillars and amphibious creatures upset my parents and my teachers, even though I released the insects and frogs back into the environment.

By the time I was in high school, my mother tolerated my two pet salamanders, Sally and Mandy. They lived in a terrarium in my bedroom where the insects they required for food were not available. I collected flies from windowsills and dangled them over the terrarium on a silver spoon. The salamanders quickly learned that the flash of the spoon meant food; they happily *caught* the flies and thrived.

What I learned from all this was that life and the universe were leading me in the direction that was right for me, that I needed to persevere, and that my stubbornness, or rather, determination would help me face many challenges. When I completed high school and began university, these learnings were invaluable. Spending most of my time studying had left me socially inexperienced, unhealthy, and physically unfit. In addition, a learning disability in arithmetic, *dyscalculia*, made me wary of math courses.

Accordingly, I chose an Honors English program for my first year. I was sixteen years old, far from home, and in pre-med classes. What could go wrong? All I will say is that I learned a great deal about coping socially in that year. Assisting other students and providing tutoring helped me to succeed academically. It turns out this work was a gift that taught me about the joy of helping others. I persevered, remaining open to other messages from life that would lead me toward my goal.

The second pre-med year, I followed my love of science and animals and enrolled in Honors Zoology. The training was intense, with classes and lab work all day and studying late into the night. That year did not end well: a fellow student committed suicide. He was only seventeen

A pall fell over our group, and we wondered who might be next to succumb to the pressures of the grueling program. The pursuit of joining the medical profession had ended in tragedy for a brilliant young man. The experience left its mark, and I began to realize the importance of mental health as another signal from life and the universe.

Hundreds of students had applied to enter the Faculty of Medicine that year and 120 were accepted. I was one of them, along with ten other women. I felt both overwhelmed and ecstatically happy to be studying medicine. The professors were interesting, classes and labs were endless, and the competition was fierce; a number of students dropped out. I persevered, becoming more and more interested in health maintenance and the prevention of disease, and as a result, I became healthier and more physically fit.

The fourth and final year of medical training was the most demanding: we were put to work seeing patients on the hospital wards. Our preceptors often looked askance at the one female in their group of medical student trainees. Some expressed their frustration with our taking up a worthy male's space, wasting their time and the government's money. They presumed we would only be getting married and having children, never using our expensive training and their invaluable mentorship. Despite encountering these attitudes, all eleven women completed their medical degrees.

But the shaming for being female resulted in feeling that I never knew enough, was never good enough. While completing my internship at the hospital, I focused on studying and became a perfectionist. I rationalized this obsession by telling myself that learning was desirable. After all, wouldn't people prefer to see a doctor who was thorough and perfectionistic?

Apparently they did, as once I began practicing family medicine, my services were constantly in demand. I loved the work and put in long hours, facing many challenges and persevering. Serving others, I experienced heartfelt joy. A newborn baby opening their eyes and examining their world, patients overcoming diseases like cancer, and seniors' delighting in my two young children as I worked at retirement homes on weekends were all gifts.

But the medical system was not oriented toward prevention or cure of disease, apart from dealing with injuries and serious infections—the focus was on management of disease. What was life telling me?

After eleven years of having the privilege of serving patients as a family doctor, I had become disillusioned with the direction medicine was headed. I remembered the clues that life and the universe were providing about the importance of mental health. I applied and was accepted into a psychiatry residency. After four years of study, during which I maintained my certification in family medicine, I emerged as a fully qualified child, adolescent, and adult psychiatrist.

Had I finally reached my goal? Become the person I wanted and needed to be? The truth is that reaching higher in life comes with responsibilities. Growing to meet the challenges of helping children and families heal required support from my mentors and colleagues, as well as from life and the universe. Determination and perseverance allowed me to succeed in providing medical care to thousands of patients over more than fifty years, a gift I am grateful and privileged to have received.

Would I have experienced this gift if I had obeyed my mother's friend who said women could be nurses, not doctors? Would I have become so avidly interested in the sciences if I had placated my parents and teachers by not collecting frogs and other creatures? And would I have become a physician if I had taken to heart the rejection by medical preceptors?

I think not. But persisting despite difficulties and not allowing yourself to be discouraged by others clears your path. What signals are you receiving from life and the universe? Move toward your passion, meet challenges with determination, and be amazed by your progress.

Put your well-being first—you will need energy. Forgive yourself for allowing obstacles from the past to stand in your way. When an endeavor fails, life is providing an opportunity for you to learn and succeed. Keep going.

On this journey, remember that generosity is its own reward. When you serve with love and care, you create your greatest life. And receive your greatest gifts!

Tanya Wulff, MD. Fifty years as a physician led to Tanya's becoming a transformational life coach online. She cannot imagine a more fulfilling life than caring for others and facilitating their valuing and caring for themselves, their fellow humans, and other occupants of our incredible planet. Along with her amazing husband of fifty-two years, she is often outdoors appreciating nature. Contact her at: drtanyawulff@gmail.com

FINAL THOUGHTS

Throughout these pages, the authors of this book have shared their stories of heartbreak, inspiration, and compassion. They have chronicled lives changed in a moment, in a turning point, and described the paths forward from those moments. They have been generous and honest with us, offering the wisdom and insight gained as they traveled through events often labeled *crisis, unimaginable, challenging,* or *devastating*.

Have you, perhaps, identified your own *turning point moments?*

Most of the time, we never see the curve in the road ahead until we are navigating it, hands clutching the steering wheel. It is easy to feel isolated and alone when facing these events, but after reading the dozens of stories in *Turning Point Moments*, *Volume Two*, you can be assured that you are not alone at all. We share similar journeys of pain and loss, of hope and new life. The writers in these pages have offered you the gems of their own experience to carry with you for just such times.

All of us working on *Turning Point Moments, Volume Two* have been personally blessed by each story, each moment, and each act of courage demonstrated by these ordinary people who pushed through their struggles in extraordinary ways. We are inspired to live out their hope in the twists and turns of our own lives, and we know you have been inspired as well.

Did one or two stories stand out for you? Many of our authors have included contact information for you to share your story or to enquire about the guidance they offer through coaching, courses, and books. If their message resonates with you, we encourage you to seek out their assistance through their services and products. For in their tales, a common thread weaves in and out of these pages—we all need the support and insight of others as we navigate the curves of this life, especially in our ever-changing world.

As you move forward, we encourage you to cultivate the courage to share your own wisdom and insights gleaned from the turning point moments of your life. You, too, have unique perspectives and gifts that are needed in a world dealing with rampant individualism and fear. Do you have a story to share? A blog to post? A book to write?

We want to thank you for reading our book and for joining us in our efforts to support each other as we create a better world for us all. We are hopeful that as we round the corners of our lives, we will meet you again somewhere down the road.

DO YOU HAVE AN IDEA FOR A BOOK?

If reading these stories has inspired you to write your own book, we've got the perfect way to get started.

Our award-winning *Get Your Book Done* program has helped more than 1,000 authors in 47 countries get their book idea out of their head, onto the page, and into the world. Now it's your turn, and you can get started right now, for *free*.

Get Free Help to Write Your Book:

www.turningpointmoments.com/writemybook

NEED HELP PUBLISHING YOUR BOOK?

If you're nearly done, or already finished writing your manuscript and trying to figure out how to get your book published, we're here to help.

Capucia Publishing has been supporting authors publish life-changing, transformational books since 2004. We're an independent, author-centric publishing company with a dedicated team ready to walk you through every single step to seeing your book published and launched into the world. Our comprehensive done-for-you service easily makes your book idea a published reality.

Let's Talk About Publishing.
www.turningpointmoments.com/publish

CONNECT WITH US

Websites

www.turningpointmoments.com
www.getyourbookdone.com
www.capuciapublishing.com

Social Media

www.getyourbookdone.com/community
@christinekloser
@christinekloser

Mail

Capucia LLC
211 Pauline Drive #513
York, PA 17402

Contact

Phone: (800) 930-3713
Email: support@getyourbookdone.com